Living in the Lions' Den

Living
in the
Lions'
Den

How to Cope with
Life's Stresses

Paul L. Morell

Abingdon Press
Nashville

LIVING IN THE LIONS' DEN
How to Cope with Life's Stresses

Copyright © 1992 by Abingdon Press

This book is printed on recycled acid-free paper.

Library of Congress Cataloging-in-Publication Data

Morell, Paul L.
     Living in the lions' den: how to cope with life's stresses/Paul L. Morell.
          p.   cm.
     ISBN 0-687-22295-8 (alk. paper)
     1. Christian life—1960–   2. Stress (Psychology)—Religious aspects—Christianity. I. Title.
BV4501.2.M5835   1992
248.4—dc20   91-18020

MANUFACTURED IN THE UNITED STATES OF AMERICA

Our Lord has surrounded me with love and special people of faith all through my life. The beautiful people nearest to me today are my wife, Ann, and our three daughters—Peggy Ann, Shana Lynette, and Paula Carolyn. All of them have had a part in the preparation of this book and have been enthusiastic about the project. Their lives and related events were fertile soil for the truths that allow us to know that we *can* live in today's world (the lions' den) and survive, through God's grace.

Ann has been as fine a minister's wife as there ever could be. No task or challenge has been too hard. She has done all things well. For me, her gift of love and caring is a great blessing from God. She leads devotionals and Bible studies, and is a speaker in her own right.

Our girls have enriched our lives. Grown, they have married Christian men and are people of faith, grace, and quality wherever they go. The Church is stronger because of their labor and Godly trust. May this book bring remembrances of happy moments and never-ending relationships.

Paul L. Morell

F O R E W O R D

Sometimes I read a book, then wish I could meet the author. What are her real thoughts? What are his true feelings? To read Paul Morell is to sit down by the fire, share a cup of coffee, and chat about the ups and downs of life. No pretense, no formality—just two good friends talking softly, with long pauses.

The style is warm, friendly, conversational. But the stuff of the dialogue is deep—life and death, sickness and health, guilt and forgiveness. On his brow, furrows seem to crease as he shares the anxieties and fears, the times of loneliness and anger that plague us all. But you can almost see the smile sweep over his face as glimmers of faith and hope shine through the conversation.

Perhaps Dr. Morell is most helpful in simply sharing his "having been there." Call it empathy, call it experience, our spirits grow calmer with his reassurance that we can be victorious even in the lions' den of life's spiritual dangers. Out of his heart, his rich family life, an amazing pastoral ministry with countless personal wrestlings, he observes and shares and contemplates— but always in an open-ended way, knowing that a new encounter is just around the corner.

Paul Morell is a master of the illustration. He reaches for cartoons, whimsical stories, scriptural episodes, family intima- cies, to make his point. Just as I have already circled illustrations for my own use, so teachers and preachers, public speakers and writers will quickly do the same.

His insights seem to have been nurtured by Scripture. The very source of reconciliation and courage, of optimism and victorious living is woven into the tapestry of this book—a deep and lively faith in God, confirmed in everyday experience. The references to religion are neither pompous nor pious, but rather make practical, wise, courageous living a natural outcome from a deep and committed faith.

The dialogue is fortified in an unusual way. Questions—introspective exams—pull the reader into participation. The reader will respond, answer, add to the conversation. Rather than simply listening to counsel or gathering information, readers will find their minds racing down the avenues of personal experience, rooting out resentment, letting go of the excess baggage of guilt or fear, reprioritizing time or money.

So *Living in the Lions' Den* is not only interesting reading, it is a guide to growth, an experience in faith projection, a help in learning to walk tall and straight, like the mighty prophet Daniel himself.

Richard B. Wilke

C O N T E N T S

The Lions of Stress

Are You Devoured, or Delivered?

The Christmas of 1983 was one I will never forget. It was the Christmas our family was "on the move." Even Santa couldn't find us!

My wife and I were in the process of moving across Dallas to a different church and a new parsonage—we hoped, in time for Christmas. But this possibility became less likely as each day passed.

Unusually mild Texas temperatures had plummeted to record-breaking below-freezing lows, which included ice and snow. The electricity (of most interest, the heat) couldn't be turned on in our new home until the building met inspection, and it couldn't meet inspection until the builder complied with city codes. And because there was no heat, the pipes froze and the house flooded.

The list of frustrating problems continued to escalate. To top it off, our oldest daughter lay in the hospital recuperating from major surgery, and her husband and children were in town temporarily. Our middle daughter and her family were arriving any day from North Carolina, and our youngest daughter would be returning from university for Christmas vacation. We had planned a big family Christmas, and now had no inn where we could celebrate, or even lay our heads!

Realizing that we would not be able to move into our new home in time for Christmas, the members of our church graciously began to open their homes to us. So the entire tribe—three daughters, two sons-in-law, three grandchildren, and my wife and I—descended on an unsuspecting member's home. Can you imagine how much stuff we carried with us? What a sight we must have been! Certainly not the sophisticated suburban clergy family.

For ten days our family shivered and shook, slipped and slid from house to house. On Christmas Sunday, as we were making the supreme effort to get to our church to make a good first impression, the car was too cold to start, and as we headed for the member's house to call for the needed help, we realized we were locked out! Neighbors saw us climbing through a window and thought we were trying to break in! Christmas Day behind bars was not our goal.

The year continued from bad to worse. I was attempting to lead a new flock of three thousand church members who were hesitant about being led. My wife, Ann, had her hands full trying to make our new house a home (we finally moved in on New Year's Eve), caring for her step-mother and very ill father, and finding her new niche in our church. There were two family deaths. Then our oldest daughter, Patty, underwent a second major surgery, along with a series of minor ones, and her health became a constant source of concern. As if that weren't enough, our youngest daughter, Paula, began to have physical problems which resulted in two serious surgeries.

Everywhere we turned, we met a new and hungry lion. Life in the lions' den was no fun; it was unpleasant, stressful, and just plain wretched at times. We wanted to get out, to seek refuge somewhere. I prayed for help, for quick answers and relief, but it seemed my prayers were not being answered. God was strangely silent.

Do any of these situations sound familiar? Have you experienced seasons of living right in the den with the lions? If we are honest, we all must admit to times when life becomes a mad struggle, a vicious entanglement with the circumstances of this world.

The Lions of Stress

As I write these lines, dens of lions may be stalking some families. I have known of several families that have been attacked. A mother once told me that her daughter had been arrested. She said, "I am actually relieved, because in jail she may be safe from drugs and suicide." Wives and children in many homes live in utter fear of a drunken husband or father and his regular beatings. I have known other husbands and fathers who are confined to wheelchairs; other children who are shuffled like cards between divorced parents. And there is still excruciating agony for families in which children have been molested.

In these desperately painful situations, the den seems more like a dungeon, and we begin to believe that we already have been devoured. We experience spiritual claustrophobia. How can we gain hope from God to deal with our troublesome—or devastating—circumstances?

The story of Daniel in the Bible deals directly with the way one person managed to live in a lions' den without being devoured. Daniel's ability to trust God completely in the midst of severe circumstances merits a second look on our part. The setting of the story takes us back into history thousands of years ago, to the kingdom of the Medes and Persians. Highly intelligent young Daniel has been brought as a Jewish exile to the capital city of Babylonia, where he has been trained to serve Darius, the king. Daniel so distinguished himself among the other trainees by his amazing abilities that the king put him in sole charge of the kingdom. The other rulers became jealous of Daniel's rapid ascendancy and began to look for faults in his character. But they could find no corruption in him.

However, they did discover one unique thing which he continued to do: Three times a day, he knelt toward Jerusalem and prayed to the God of Abraham, Isaac, and Jacob—the God of his fathers. The rulers realized that this prayerful habit could be Daniel's downfall, so they set up a foolproof plan to trap him. First, they advised King Darius to decree that during the next thirty days, anyone who prayed to any god except the king would be thrown into the lions' den. Then they sat back and waited for Daniel to transgress the new law.

Daniel was undaunted by the new edict. He continued to go to his upstairs room three times a day and kneel in prayer before his open window, "giving thanks to his God, *just as he had done before*" (Dan. 6:10 NIV, italics mine). Daniel trusted God implicitly.

Daniel's outward circumstances continued to worsen. The other rulers caught Daniel praying and told the king of his disobedience. King Darius knew he must put Daniel into the lions' den to uphold his royal word. So Daniel, *a faithful servant of God,* was thrown into the lions' den—a sure death in the eyes of the world.

How did God help Daniel in his life-threatening situation? It seems to me that the important message here is not, "Where was God during this time?" but "Where was *Daniel* in his relationship with God during this time?" We discover from the story that although Daniel vividly experienced a night in the lions' den, he was not devoured. He remained safe and secure because he continued to trust God completely, even in the midst of his circumstances. To Daniel, *trust meant complete confidence in God's faithfulness and integrity.*

What strong comparisons we can see between the lions' den we frequently experience in today's world, and the den where Daniel was cast! We, too, have faced circumstances which seemed difficult if not impossible. God may not spare us from being cast to the lions, but he can surround us with protective grace in the den. As we call upon God, we too can be delivered from the lions' mouths and remain safe. We can emerge from the experience just as Daniel did—wiser, more thankful, and more aware of our dependence upon a faithful God.

Can we learn to continue to pray and to trust God, even when the nights spent with the lions stretch into weeks, months, even years? Can we learn to ask not, "Where is *God?*" but "Where am

I in my relationship with God?" If so, amidst our trials, in the thick of the lions' den of life, we can actually emerge with a stronger faith and a life full of peace and joy.

As we learn to trust God in the midst of our trials, we also can discover useful ways of lessening the impact of the stresses which bombard our lives. Learning to cope with the stresses that come our way, while continuing to grow in faith, is what this book is about. In a greater way, this is what the Christian life is about. May we embark on an adventure to discover Christlike ways to manage the everyday, and the not so everyday stresses of life.

The Lion of Busyness
Stressed Up, Down, and Out!

PERSONAL INVENTORY: Are you too busy?

Fill in the blanks with a Yes or No answer to the following questions:

_____ 1. I am usually in a hurry.

_____ 2. I am often late for appointments and meetings.

_____ 3. I try to accomplish more in one day than time allows.

_____ 4. I don't stop to smell the roses.

_____ 5. I continually promise myself that I will get organized "tomorrow."

_____ 6. I find it difficult to turn down a volunteer job and feel guilty if I do, especially a job at the church or in Christian circles.

_____ 7. I don't spend enough time with my family.

_____ 8. I feel indispensable to many organizations—if I don't do the job, no one will.

_____ 9. My work schedule takes priority over all personal concerns.

_____10. I plan to slow my life down soon.

Give yourself 5 points for a Yes answer and 0 points for a No answer. Total all points.

1-10 points—You're probably not being honest!

15-20 points—You're doing a pretty good job of organizing your priorities and living life to its fullest.

20-30 points—You could use some help in reorganizing priorities and slowing down your obligations.

35-50 points—Help! You're drowning in busyness!

WHY DOESN'T A WEEK HAVE EIGHT DAYS?

I was still getting dressed one morning when my phone rang at 6:45. On the other end of the line, a church member said gently, "Brother Paul, I hate to bother you at this hour of the morning, but my husband passed away a few hours ago." I listened to the details, anguished and prayed with her, and promised to visit later in the morning. I quickly finished dressing, downed some breakfast, and headed out the door. I had a feeling it was going to be a difficult and busy day.

When I walked into my office, I was armed with my ever-trusted calendar in one hand and an enormous stack of papers in the other. I tossed the papers on my desk and headed for my chair to collapse briefly and study my obligations for the day.

It was only 8:00 A.M., and I was already feeling pushed! Yesterday's mail lay beckoning on my desk. Another crisis call awaited my attention. The weekly staff meeting would begin shortly. I needed to organize the visitation calls I wanted to make that evening. Several very ill members were in the hospital. I wanted time to rethink last Sunday's sermon before I started on the upcoming message. I mustn't forget the promised visit to the parishioner who had called that morning. And the following morning, I was leaving town to attend the quarterly board meeting for a national mission society.

I had to employ only minimal thinking skills to realize that I would need about thirty-five hours to complete even the priority items in my schedule. Since I would have only half that time, I began consciously to shift my responsibilities into a time frame that would fit into the real world. Every day my schedule seems to become more complex! Pastoring a large suburban Dallas church is an awesome task, and I often feel there are not enough months in the year, days in the week, or hours in the day to accomplish the work to which I feel God has called me.

Many of you are no different. Most of us operate on overload. Living in America at the end of the twentieth century seems to be synonymous with a hectic life-style! Rapidly expanding technology in the areas of communication and transportation foster an unbelievable volume of cafeteria-style choices for ways we can spend our working and nonworking hours. Wherever we work, our job beckons for more of our attention. And our nonworking hours become a mad array of time-juggling activities to enhance our physical appearance and further our emotional relationships. Even churches have entered the competitive arena of where and how our time will be spent!

Scrambled schedules produce harried life-styles which cause stress. Psychologists tell us we need to reduce stress by simplifying our lives, slowing down, taking it easy. Time-management experts advise us to become better organized, to form goals and set daily schedules. The church offers its solution by calling us to set priorities (coyly assuming that *it* will be the number-one priority!).

How can we deal with hectic schedules and have any time left for the "Lord's work"? How can we juggle the hours in our day so that we have time for the "more important things" in life? How can we spend more time with our spouse, children, and other loved ones and friends? What is it that *really* counts in our lives, as we seek to do God's will on this earth?

These questions are important. In fact, because we *are* Christians, the lion of busyness may be even bigger in our lives than it is in the lives of non-Christians, because of our overriding priorities. It may be bigger because . . .

- we consciously seek the will of God in every aspect of our lives;
- we do not want to neglect the needs of our local church;
- we wish to remain true to our individual callings;
- we desire to develop our God-given gifts;
  and
- we emphasize the importance of particular responsibilities in marital and parental relationships.

In fact, I'll go so far as to say (and I'm sure you will agree with me) that the lion of busyness can be one of the most crippling problems Christians face in our day. However, it can be turned into a creative challenge, if we can first recognize the problem and then begin to get a handle on it.

RECOGNIZING THE PROBLEM

A popular bumper sticker of a few years back expressed our dilemma exactly: Don't follow me—I'm lost!

Often we don't know what the problem is, and thus we can't even begin to deal with it. The problem is so cultural that we can whiz through our existence on planet Earth without realizing that we have missed the abundant life offered by our Savior Jesus Christ.

On the interstate highway between Dallas and Houston, there is a family graveyard from the previous century. Probably no one ever notices it as they speed by. In fact, my daughter and her husband (who make the trip numerous times throughout the year) never would have noticed it, had they not left the freeway for a "pit-stop." As they headed down a less traveled road adjacent to the highway, they noticed the twenty or so tombstones—a mere twelve feet from the outside freeway lane—slightly hidden behind a group of trees. Because they had slowed their pace for a brief moment, they were able to share a quiet place of dignity.

How many times do we miss the true meaning of life because we are preoccupied with less important things? Jesus said, "The thief comes only to steal and kill and destroy; I came that they may have life, and have it abundantly" (John 10:10). Let's recognize that busyness has the capacity to weary us so that we become ineffective. But the good news is this: Once we discover the problem, we can move from the position of crippled servers to creative servants.

PRIORITIES: WHO NEEDS THEM?

The musical *Fiddler on the Roof* enjoyed great popularity. One of the songs, "Sunrise, Sunset," reflects on the all-too-sure passage of time in this life. Quickly, the days become the years that bring a child to adulthood. Each little child becomes tall and can no longer be carried. "Swiftly flow the days," and once past, they cannot be relived.

Nearly all of us need to rethink our priorities. Will you rethink your priorities? If so, good! You are not beyond help!

Did you score too many points on the Personal Inventory at the beginning of the chapter? It's O.K.! At least you recognize your problem—a necessary beginning for meaningful life.

Now let's move from a recognition of the problem to finding some solutions. It's time to begin to tame the lion of busyness!

Find a blank sheet of paper, or better yet, a spiral notebook. Title the first sheet: Ideal Priorities. What persons or things are most important in your life? List your priorities in order of importance. This will take a little thought—you'd better use a pencil with a good eraser!

As you consider and rethink what is important in your life, you might want to reflect upon the following meditations:

Therefore do not be anxious, saying, "What shall we eat?" or "What shall we drink?" or "What shall we wear?" For the Gentiles seek all these things; and your heavenly Father knows that you need them all. But seek first his kingdom and his righteousness, and all these things shall be yours as well. (Matt. 6:31-33)

It is in vain that you rise up early and go late to rest, eating the bread of anxious toil;
   for he gives to his beloved sleep. (Ps. 127:2)

Have this mind among yourselves, which is yours in Christ Jesus, who, though he was in the form of God, did not count equality with God a thing to be grasped, but emptied himself, taking the form of a servant, being born in the likeness of men. And being found in human form he humbled himself and became obedient unto death, even death on a cross. (Phil. 2:5-8)

Therefore a man leaves his father and his mother and cleaves to his wife, and they become one flesh. (Gen. 2:24)

And they were bringing children to him, that he might touch them; and the disciples rebuked them. But when Jesus saw it he was indignant, and said to them, "Let the children come to me, do not hinder them; for to such belongs the kingdom of God. Truly, I say to you, whoever does not receive the kingdom of God like a child shall not enter it." And he took them in his arms and blessed them, laying his hands upon them. (Mark 10:13-16)

After listing your ideal priorities in order of importance, take out a new sheet of paper or start a new page in your notebook. Also, get out your calendar for the past year (or any schedule book you may have). If you do not have anything that would reflect how your time has been spent over the last year, you will need to remember! Title this second page: Actual Priorities. Now determine and write down the five areas on which you have spent most time during the last year.

Title a third page: Weekly Priorities. Think back to your schedule for the past week. Write down any activities in which you have been involved for an hour or more. Total up the approximate hours you have spent in these activities, and note the time beside each one.

Now look back over the ideal priorities you listed. Compare these with the ways you have actually spent your time over the last year and week. Are your lists of Actual Priorities and Weekly Priorities strikingly similar to your Ideal Priorities? Or are they radically different? Are you spending your time pursuing activities you feel are important? Or are you putting your time into countless activities of lesser importance, while your ideal priorities are neglected?

If you answer Yes to those questions, you need to begin reorganizing your time to serve your ideal priorities. For example, when I compared my lists, I discovered how often I allow interruptions to invade my devotional and sermon-preparation time, and how easy it is for me to overlook my family as I pursue church-related activities.

How did I begin to help myself? How can you start reorganizing your time to better reflect the priorities you have chosen? Read on!

REORGANIZING YOUR PRIORITIES

You may say,

_____ "I don't know how to reorganize my priorities."

_____ "No matter what I do, I meet myself coming and going."

_____ "There are so many good things that need to be done!"

_____ "If I don't do it, it won't get done."

_____ "No one else can do it quite as well as I can."

All these excuses sound good. But they keep the lion of busyness's jaw cocked.

There are ways to relax that lion's jaw! One of the best ways is to *minimize the nonessential things in your life.* In other words, just say No!

Several years ago my eldest daughter was going through a crisis of defining the priorities in her life. She went to her minister to discuss the problem, and he responded by saying simply, "Patty, you are trying to sell your talents for a dime. Get rid of the things in your life that threaten your obedience to God's calling. There always will be many good things wooing you and vying for your time. So it's very important for you to choose carefully where you will spend your time as you pursue your God-given ministry."

We all need to reevaluate our priorities. It's important to recheck where we are spending the majority of our time.

How can you do this? First, set a timetable to follow as you start unloading the unnecessary baggage of a too-hectic life. Ask yourself, "Does this activity fit into the priorities I have set for my life?" If not, get rid of it, if at all possible. If you absolutely can't get rid of it, look for ways to minimize the time demand it places on you.

While you are unloading current baggage, don't take on any new loads. Place copies of your Ideal Priorities list by the telephone, on your desk at work, and in your billfold. Before you accept any new duties, ask yourself if this new obligation fits into the new priorities you have set for your life. Does this new demand move you further along the road of your God-given calling, or does it keep you from important goals in your life? If you are not sure, talk it over with your spouse or a dear friend. Bring the matter before God in prayer to seek wisdom. Don't glibly accept new responsibilities that are nothing more than a meaningless waste of your time.

A second way to relax that lion's jaw and lessen your busyness is to *realize that you cannot do everything.* David A. Seamands tells a story about a young woman who came to him for counseling. She became very emotional as she heaped failure upon failure on herself. She described her existence as "living on the nub." Dr. Seamands says that after he had listened to her, he leaned forward and spoke eagerly:

> "Angela, may I touch you?"
> She looked startled and backed away from me. "What?"
> Again I asked her, "May I touch you? You see, it's been a long time since I've seen such a divine being."
> "What do you mean?"
> "What I mean, Angela, is that only some kind of godlike creature could expect to do all the things you listed, let alone do them perfectly. You have absolutely divine expectations. Where did you ever get the notion that you or anyone else were expected to do all those things? What I hear you saying is that you feel guilty because you can't do everything and do it flawlessly!"[1]

Many of us are the same way! We try to do anything and everything, and then we wonder why we feel frustrated so much of the time!

We have many reasons to justify being so involved. Often, our ego is boosted when we feel that we are important to so many people or organizations. We even pride ourselves on being busy—certainly no one can accuse us of being lazy! We like to believe we are indispensable, that no one is quite capable of taking our place. We think the organization will fail, or be somewhat less, without our input or assistance.

At other times, we try to do too many things because we feel we will "let God down" or neglect our church, business, or family, and there are myriad other pseudo guilt trips we put on ourselves.

What we need to realize is that when we give up a chance to be involved in an organization or to minister to others, we allow someone else to exercise his or her special talents or abilities. We need to bury our pride or our guilt—as the case may be—and give others a chance to fulfill their calling. Every person needs a chance to experience God's blessing in service.

The apostle Paul practiced this philosophy as he instructed Timothy: "What you have heard from me before many witnesses entrust to faithful men who will be able to teach others also" (II Tim. 2:2). When we can see one of our primary goals in life as that of enabling others to use their gifts for the service and glory of God, we have learned one more way to simplify our hectic lives.

ON THE PERSONAL SIDE

You may wonder how I have begun to apply these suggestions to my own life. First, I have managed to minimize some of the nonessentials in my life by carefully planning my schedule. I have found that my secretary can and will handle more of my phone calls, if I will allow her to do so. The other ministers on my staff can and will help with many of my duties, if I will so instruct them. In this way I can concentrate on my greatest gifts; my thoughts become less scattered; my plans, more cohesive. And I am aware that when I am willing to let go of those few things that unnecessarily jumble my day, I allow others a chance to minister, and at the same time, I remain more true to my special talents and calling.

I also am trying to give more of my time to my wife and my youngest daughter, who lives in the Dallas area. I eat lunch with my wife when possible; and once a week, I take my daughter to lunch. I am making a greater effort to visit my out-of-town daughters and their families more frequently. I notice that the value-setting I have done has given me a better opportunity to focus on my family and fulfill the important priorities I have set.

Life is short, but oh, how exciting it can be! Why not choose to move toward a simpler and more fulfilling life-style?

The Lion of Busyness

DO YOU REALLY WANT TO SMELL THE ROSES?

As in anything, balance is important. God has given us talents to use; we dare not be idle. However, we need to evaluate our time goals and diligently see that our activities line up with our calling. We must learn to eliminate the less important things and minimize the others. We can revel in watching others take to the sky as we help to prepare them for their many avenues of service. We can rest in the peace of focusing on the things of first importance.

Practice makes perfect! It takes time to learn to hurry less, smell the roses more, and peacefully walk with the Lord. The effort is worth it! When we evaluate our priorities, reorganize them, and seek to settle our busy hearts, we will receive the waiting rewards of peace and joy.

ELEVEN WAYS TO TAME THE LION OF BUSYNESS

1. Recognize busyness for what it is: a lion that wishes to devour you. Make conscious plans to protect yourself so that you are not easy prey.
2. Set realistic goals for yourself by prioritizing. Eliminate those activities at the bottom of your list.
3. Begin each day by reviewing your "game plan" with Jesus. Five minutes of reflection upon what is important may bless you more than you know.
4. Have a time for Scripture and prayer. Be disciplined.
5. Don't take on too much. Normally, a Christian should not take on more than one major and one minor responsibility in church, beyond worship and Sunday school (small group) involvement. You might have a community service project. The rest of the time belongs to your family, unexpected emergencies, and essential current commitments.

27

6. Limit the activities in which your children participate. They cannot be gone from home *all* the time. Home, school, and church responsibilities are important to teach them a balanced life.
7. Learn to stay home—don't go out of town every other weekend. Most of us do not need a second home at the nearby lake, the beach, or the mountains. Use some of the money you save by staying at home for God's concerns.
8. Get adequate rest. Don't make yourself a loser before you begin your day.
9. The sabbath principle is sound. Ease up one day a week.
10. Avoid debt whenever possible. Don't buy what you can't afford. (I'll deal with this more in chapter 3.)
11. Discover simple ways to spend leisure time with your family and friends.

(For additional reading suggestions for each chapter, see "More Food for Thought," beginning on page 151.)

JOURNAL JOTS

For Fun: If I could choose the number of hours that should be in one day, I would choose _____. Why? _____

_____

_____

For Discovery: Jesus was a firm believer in setting priorities for his time. One of the best ways for us to choose our values is to follow the instructions in Matthew 6:33-35. Summarize Jesus' instructions: _____

_____

_____

He, whose very life was ministry, also set aside time to receive ministry. See Mark 1:35; 3:13-17; Luke 11:1-4. What can we learn from Jesus' example? _____

_____

_____

For Commitment This Week: Before I take on any new obligations this week, I will ask for God's wisdom as I consider whether this obligation fits into my established goals.
My decision: _____

_____

_____

29

The Lion of Career

Having God for Boss

PERSONAL INVENTORY: How do you feel about your work?

1. Rank the following occupations from 1 to 10, in order of importance to the community:

_____ minister	_____ secretary
_____ doctor	_____ bank executive
_____ attorney	owner of a small
_____ preschool teacher	_____ business
_____ college professor	_____ salesperson
	_____ city employee

2. Which of the following factors do you think one should consider before choosing a particular career? Place a + beside those factors you feel are imperative to consider; a ? beside somewhat important factors; an X beside the factors you think should not be considered.

personal	personal
_____ enjoyment	_____ satisfaction
_____ salary	training/
encouragement	education
_____ from friends/family	_____ needed

	amount of travel		flexibility of
_____	involved	_____	schedule
	influence on	_____	prestige
_____	others' lives		response to
		_____	God's call

3. I feel that God can best be served in the following occupation: _____

EENIE, MEENIE, MYNIE, MOO, TELL ME, GOD, JUST WHAT TO DO.

I consider myself one of the fortunate ones. I've never had to flounder in search of God's calling for my life. I knew unequivocally, at the ripe old age of fifteen, that God was calling me into the ministry. I never have doubted that call, either then or today.

Oh, it's true that I did try to bargain with God at first. I attended a youth camp at the Turner Falls Methodist encampment in Oklahoma. As I felt the first tugs of God's Spirit moving me toward the pastoral ministry, I reasoned with God that I would consider being a Sunday school *teacher*.

But one Sunday night in late July, our pastor at St. Luke's Methodist Church in Oklahoma City spoke about the great power of the atomic bomb—a tremendous power with destructive capabilities. He challenged us to accept the power of God in our lives—a tremendous power, but with *constructive* capacities. Following the service, the youth group met in a Starlight Time in the backyard of one of the church members. Again, God wooed me to "go where the line was thinnest." I knew in my heart that God was calling me to the ordained ministry. In that occupation, I could use God's power for

31

redemptive purposes in the world. I had discovered human need, and I decided I wanted to make a difference, with God's help.

YOUR OCCUPATION: A JOB? OR A CALLING?

I realize that not everyone has the same experience toward a clear-cut calling. While many of you may have felt an unmistakable call to a specific career, others may be seeking, or feel unsure of, God's guidance in the area of your career. *Do not be ashamed or think less of yourself if this is the case!* There are ways you can discover the call of God on your life! To do this, you may need to choose an occupation, change occupations, or simply learn how to view your job differently.

Many Christian teenagers and young adults really suffer when they begin to seek God's guidance toward a career. Part of the problem stems from a wrong idea that many of them have been taught—that there is one, and only one, career that God has planned for them. As a result of this popular teaching, they frantically seek "God's will" for their lives by first asking, and later begging, God to divulge this "secret."

Several problems arise with this way of thought. First, the character of God is defamed by this outlook, because God is made to look like a rather malicious person who gets some sort of perverted delight from watching human subjects struggle with answers which God may or may not reveal. Second, this idea minimizes a person's talents by assuming that there is only one perfect career that will utilize his or her talents in an appropriate way. Third, this way of thinking elevates a career to a utopian status, making a young person think that a career can satisfy all his or her needs and the needs of others, when in reality, only a right relationship with Jesus Christ can do that.

What, then, *is* the way to seek God's will for our lives? If you are a person seeking to find your "calling," what steps can you take to discover God's guidance in your career choice?

First of all, in seeking to make your career a calling and not just a job, *begin to determine how your talents best meet human need.* How do you see your particular strengths or talents juxtapositioning with human need? Where do these two—talent and need—intermingle? The place you can put your talent to work serving God and God's people—this is where to begin discovering the call of God on your life.

Let's suppose you are a person who is seeking God's calling for your life. Three ways can help you find out where your talents touch human need:

- Prayer
- Introspection
- Christian counsel.

How can prayer help you discover your calling? In the words of James Montgomery, "Prayer is the simplest form of speech that infant lips can try; prayer the sublimest strains that reach the Majesty on high."[1] Proverbs 16:3 says, "Commit your work to the LORD, and your plans will be established." The words of Paul to the church at Philippi remind us to "not worry about anything, but in everything by prayer and supplication with thanksgiving let your requests be made known to God" (Phil. 4:6). Prayer allows us to communicate our concerns to our parent whom Jesus often called Father. The One who made us can help us to see our talents and the needs of the world in a new light.

God wants to hear about our career concerns. We merely need to communicate to our Lord in a time of prayer that we want God's will for our lives in the area of our career, for the sole purpose of serving and glorifying God to the best of our ability.

Introspection, or self-examination, allows you to constructively consider what your talents are, and how you can best offer them in service to the Kingdom. Whether you are young or an older person, you can do the following simple exercise. You will not complete this exercise in one hour or a few days; it will be an ongoing project as you pray, reflect, and counsel. Take out a sheet of paper (or your spiral notebook). Divide the sheet into two columns: My Talents and Human Need. Begin with the My Talents column. List every talent you think you possess, whether it be something innate (such as an attitude or a God-given gift) or something external (such as a way of relating to others, or a strength you have worked at judiciously).

I am aware of two small but important talents I possess. One of them relates to money. I've always liked to work with it! (Of course, who doesn't?) I like to stretch it, to see how far it will go, to see how much mileage I can get out of my dollar. How important it is for a preacher to do much with little in this area! I soon learned that people often didn't contribute at all, or they put the church last on their list of financial priorities. I have had many opportunities to put this talent to the test!

I've also always loved challenges. Give me an impossible situation, and I'll try to move it within the realm of possibility. God specializes in the impossible. Maybe I'm just plain ignorant, but I'll try almost anything once! Paul said, "I can do all things through Christ who strengthens me." While a seminary student, I was sent to a three-church circuit which had had four preachers in two years. I guess my love for the formidable explains why the bishop gave me my first appointment in a distant location, with no church and few eager souls!

Most people can think of at least one area where they are relatively strong, but if you cannot think of even *one* strong point, ask help from someone in your family or a close friend who would be honest. In what areas do they see you strongest? Where do your strengths lie?

Many times, it is helpful to take an aptitude test if you are unsure of your talents. Such a test contains many questions about your interests and will show you which types of occupations would best fit your interests and training. Many college placement offices or community centers offer this type of testing at little or no cost.

After you have determined your stronger points and areas of skill, move on to the Human Need column. In what areas has your conscience been the most pricked? Where do you feel the most concern? For what or whom are your tears of agony spent? What motivates you? What gets your interest? What are your dreams?

To answer these questions, you will need to consider them patiently and prayerfully. You also may want to become involved in a church project for the needy, to see how your talents can help. Read the newspapers carefully. Jot down areas where you see the greatest human need.

While you are meshing your talents with areas of human need, you can begin to seek Christian counsel. Your pastor or someone on your church staff can help you evaluate your strengths in relation to human need. In addition to your pastor, ask your close friends and family to help you become more aware of your talents as they relate to human need. You may want also to seek the advice of a trained Christian counselor.

It is appropriate to consider what will pay a living wage. Doing good, or being a Christian, does not require that we lack food on the table all the time. Often, where there is a shortage of workers or quality employees, wages can be higher. When other factors are nearly even, one should consider income in the choice of vocation. In fact, the wage may be a serious indication of the opportunity and need that ought to be met by the Christian.

Finally, after you have prayed and reflected on your own talents as they relate to human need and sought the help of trusted friends and family, rethink your list. Continue to compare the two columns. Are you beginning to see places where your talents coincide with human need? Don't hesitate to get much good counsel at this point.

GET ON WITH IT!

Once you have matched your talents with human need, *find out how you can prepare yourself for careers in these areas. Move forward decisively! Dare to dream!*

I began to gather and sharpen my skills shortly after I made the decision to become a pastor. My senior year in high school, I joined the debate team. I soon realized that I was gifted at extemporaneous speaking. When I entered Oklahoma City University the next fall, I joined the debate team and traveled across the South, even chalking up a few wins! By the time I arrived at Southern Methodist University in Dallas, I was sought-after material! The much-needed groundwork for extemporaneous speaking was being laid!

Noted pastor and author Charles L. Allen once told a story about a wild duck. This duck could fly high and far, and one day he landed in a barnyard. There life was less exciting, but easier. The duck began to eat and live with the tame ducks, and gradually he forgot how to fly. He became fat and lazy.

In the spring and fall, however, as the wild ducks flew overhead, something stirred within him, but he could not rise to join them. A poem about this duck ends with these lines:

> He's a pretty good duck for the shape he's in,
> But he isn't the duck that he might have been.

Many of us have been so busy sitting around waiting for God to "tell us what to do" with our lives that we have neglected to cultivate our talents and develop our skills. Too many times we say we are waiting for God, when in reality we are searching for excuses to help us postpone career choices. Often God waits for us to begin preparation toward our career interests under the umbrellas of prayer and wise counsel. It is never too early (or too late!) to start nurturing our strengths and building our skills in preparation for a career.

Preparation may involve attending college or trade school. It may mean making sacrifices to attend graduate school. We may need to gain experience as we work our way up the employment ladder. We may need to be willing to take some chances and make some mistakes. The only fatal mistake we can make is to fail to pick ourselves up after we fall! *Remember: Christians get up one more time than they are knocked down.* Choose your goal, and begin to work toward it!

Throughout our preparation period, we should continually pray for wisdom and guidance, being thankful to God for the freedom and myriad choices we have. Some people are single-minded—they seem to know God's call with certainty. But others, after prayerfully asking for God's guidance, need to move from being paralyzed with fear and indecision, toward walking forward with hope and resolution.

GETTING TO THE TOP

Once you pass the crisis of securing a meaningful occupation, a new lion cub rears its head. The job starts to become paramount in your life. Much of your time and energy is directed toward improving yourself in your occupation and making the business more successful. This is not bad in itself, for you should want to do your best. However, when your focus begins to move from "How do I discover my calling?" to "How do I move up the ladder of success?" you may need to set guidelines to help keep your calling in its proper perspective.

One of the best ways to keep career success in line is to *remember your order of priorities* (reexamine the priorities you established in chapter 1). A cartoon illustration of Charlie Brown and his friend Lucy reminds us of what is really important in life. As they sit together in a large chair in the living room, they speak simultaneously. Of course, neither is listening to the other:

CHARLIE BROWN	LUCY
"And in the region, there were shepherds out in the field, keeping watch over their flock by night."	"I haven't bought anything for my brother's Christmas yet."
"And an angel of the Lord appeared to them."	"Everything costs so much."
"And the glory of the Lord shone around them."	"I don't want to spend a lot."
"And they were filled with fear."	"Actually, I don't want to spend any money at all."
"And the angel said to them . . ."	"I wonder if I can get him something that's free."
With that last comment, Charlie Brown falls back into the chair, Bible over his face.	"Is that it? I always thought the Christmas story was longer than that."

How often do we allow our perspective about our career to become warped? How many times do we let our priorities get out of order? Just who is our boss, anyhow?

A public opinion study in Louis Harris's *Inside America* showed that the number of hours the average American spends at work each week has increased from 40.6 in 1973 to 48.8 in 1988. In other words, since 1973, the number of hours worked by Americans has increased by 20 percent, while the amount of leisure time available to the average person has dropped 32 percent. Harris says:

This trend toward longer work hours and shorter leisure time runs counter to all the predictions that were made 10 to 20 years ago, when it was widely assumed that automation and technology would shorten the workweek and would give most people more and more leisure time. Precisely the opposite has happened.[2]

As our careers develop and become more successful and our financial obligations become more pressing, we can spend more time making money and moving along in our career than we might wish. If we are not careful, it's easy to be sucked into the entrapment of career, just as dust is sucked into a vacuum cleaner. We need to protect our leisure time by saying No to unnecessary career tasks, even if they seem important at the time. We must constantly reevaluate the way our time is spent, so that we allow time for our first priorities—God, church, and family. Our career choices must assure that our work is redemptive for us, and for our family, friends, and society.

Not only do we need to monitor the daily time we spend pursuing our career, we also must *avoid the pitfall of greed.* We have a love/hate relationship with the philosophy that *no matter how much you make, you can always use more.* Society bombards us with reasons to have money, and we are told that the more we have, the better. A dominant theme of the 1980s has been to "make it fast, make it now, get it all."[3] Every time we turn on the television or radio, we are blasted with the glamour that materialism offers. When we drive down the street, we see and smell, and even feel the tantalizing lure of what money can buy. Society tells us that money can't buy everything, but it can sure come close!

Many people remind us that the problem of greed is evident everywhere. We spend too much. Troubles caused by overconsumption and unbridled desires confront us as we go through life. We cannot afford our life-styles.

Is debt drowning you? Have you limited your opportunities

because of debt? Bill Cosby playfully discussed our problem in his book *Fatherhood:*

> A parent quickly learns that no matter how much money you have, you will never be able to buy your kids everything they want. If Snoopy doesn't send you to the poorhouse, Calvin Klein will direct the trip.[4]

Many of us want to say, "Well, greed is an issue for those who aren't Christians. Persons who have dedicated their lives to Christ and live under his authority won't struggle with the problem of greed." Unfortunately, and maybe shamelessly for us as Christians, often we are right in there on top of the greed pile with the rest of the crowd. Many of us allow our material aspirations to dominate our lives; therefore, making a lot of money becomes very important. (We'll discuss this further in chapter 3.)

So how do we cope with the glitter of success and corporate ladder-climbing? How can we keep the pursuit of material things in its proper perspective? The book of Proverbs (italics mine) gives us alternatives to our ever-seeking desire for wealth:

> Happy is the man who finds *wisdom*,
>   and the man who gets *understanding*,
> for the gain from it is better than gain from silver
>   and its profit better than gold.
> She is more precious than jewels,
>   and nothing you desire can compare with her. (3:13-15)

> Take my *instruction* instead of silver,
>   and *knowledge* rather than choice gold. (8:10)

> Riches do not profit in the day of wrath,
>   but *righteousness* delivers from death. (11:4)

> Better is a little with the *fear of the* LORD
>   than great treasure and trouble with it. (15:16)

> Better is a dinner of herbs where *love* is
>   than a fatted ox and hatred with it. (15:17)

It is better to be of a *lowly spirit* with the poor
   than to divide the spoil with the proud. (16:19)

A *good name* is to be chosen rather than great riches,
   and *favor* is better than silver or gold. (22:1)

We are responsible for our choices. May we never neglect to pursue the things of lasting importance, serving God first and foremost.

RETIREMENT:
IS THERE MORE THAN BALDNESS, BIFOCALS, BRIDGEWORK, BAY WINDOWS, AND BUNIONS?

How many times have you heard that old age is a state of mind? Here is a story that illustrates this truth:

An older woman went to see her doctor. The doctor asked her age, but she refused to tell it. Finally, the doctor said that if she would not give her age, he could not treat her, as sometimes one's age can make a difference in medication or treatment.

Reluctantly, she admitted that she was 98½.

"Now, that didn't hurt, did it?" said the doctor.

"Yes, it sure did," she replied, "for everyone thinks I am 100."

THE GOLDEN YEARS

As we enter the retirement years, or even as we begin to plan toward them, we realize that we will have additional free time. Our children will be grown, and no longer will we have work responsibilities. How can we turn our retirement years into "golden years"? How do many retired persons continue to engage in fruitful service?

To help answer these questions, let's consider Paul's words to the Colossians: "*Whatever* your task, work heartily, as serving the Lord and not men . . . you are serving the Lord Christ" (3:23-24 italics mine). We can have blessed years of retirement by continuing to faithfully *serve the Lord and others.* As we consider how our leisure time will be spent, we must plan to spend it wisely in caring for ourselves and our loved ones, and in serving our Lord through his church and people. In other words, God will always be our boss, and we are to be forever about the Lord's business!

Several years ago I had the joy of speaking to a group of retired persons called the XYZ—Extra Years of Zest. I know some of you may think that XYZ represents the end, but it doesn't need to! More than one hundred people, representing every talent that heaven has given, met together in community to plan ways to engage in meaningful expressions of their faith. Were these persons allowing the trials of old age to spoil their happiness and fruitfulness? Not on your life! They had been faithful to God, and their lives were full of the aura of Christ—the glow that comes from loving others and serving him. Their retirement years were golden years because they had the privilege of walking with the Master, and the power, love, and mercy of heaven had been poured into their lives.

Our calling and purpose in life does not stop once we reach retirement age. We may use our talents in different ways, or even discover new talents in our golden years, but we always can remain useful to ourselves, to others, and to God. The happiest senior citizens are those who spend their lives helping others.

One of my daughters directs the children's choir at her church. An older woman in the church asked if any of the children would like to learn needlepoint. Many of the children eagerly volunteered to come early or stay after rehearsals to participate in this special craft. How the children have grown to love "Mrs. Black"! They look forward to their craft time with great anticipation. And Mrs. Black, who used to walk with a cane, became so engrossed with the children that one day she left the cane at the church and has not used it again! She has a new sense of calling and purpose, and now a special interchange occurs each week between two very different generations, each giving to the other its unique talents.

I know that when I retire I will want to be busy with the work of the Lord. I imagine I will be employed as a part-time minister of evangelism in a smaller congregation, and I will continue to find great fulfillment in sharing the gospel with other folks as long as I am able.

You are never too old to share your talents with others. You are never too old to learn new jobs. You are never too old to visit others, or just to pray for others, if your health does not allow you to be ambulatory. Rejoice in your blessings and experiences, and continue to explore new roads as you walk along God's path for your life.

I WANT TO BE CALLED BY GOD.

Each of us, no matter what our age, wherever we are in life, can experience the joy and security of knowing and keeping the calling of God in our lives. Within the framework of our occupation, we can make a statement to others as to our values and priorities. We can discover that we do not live for ourselves, but to serve the Ultimate "Boss," our God. And as we serve the Lord, we get the satisfaction of making our world a little better place.

Finding our calling helps us to realize for Whom we work, to know that whatever we do, we do it for God. The ability to recognize God's call on our lives redeems our occupation from being "just a job" to a "calling." Then we can rejoice with the apostle Paul:

This one thing I do, forgetting those things which are behind, and reaching forth unto those things which are before, I press toward the mark for the prize of the high calling of God in Christ Jesus. (Phil. 3:13b-14 KJV)

JOURNAL JOTS

For Fun: The thing I like best about my job is: _____

_____

The thing I like least is: _____

_____

For Discovery: In John 5, Jesus describes his purpose and work on earth. How does your purpose compare with that of Jesus?

_____

_____

How does your occupation fit into the discovery of our purpose on earth? _____

_____

_____

For Commitment This Week: List three ways you feel you can serve God in your occupation. _____

_____

_____

_____

_____

C H A P T E R
III

The Lion of Finances
Have You Bought One Too Many Boats, Cruises, or Dream Houses?

PERSONAL INVENTORY: How much of a consumer are you?

Answer True or False to the following questions:

_____ 1. I enjoy the benefits of electricity.

_____ 2. I was born in a hospital.

_____ 3. I have indoor plumbing.

_____ 4. I live in an apartment or house.

_____ 5. I own one or more cars.

_____ 6. I have at least one TV.

_____ 7. I have a telephone.

_____ 8. I could stand to lose a few pounds.

_____ 9. I have never been without clothing. (Notice I did not say "without something to wear"!)

_____10. I have more "possessions" than I have room to store them.

Count the number of True answers.

Fewer than 5 True answers: You must be a consumer from another planet!

More than 5 True answers: You are a typical American consumer! This chapter is for you!

HOW SATISFIED ARE YOU?

My youngest daughter was married recently. In preparation for the wedding, I learned from personal experience how easy it is to become wrapped up in the American media blitz of materialism. I also rediscovered how much consumer items can cost! Let me give you some of the prices we were quoted for wedding services:

1. Wedding dress—several hundred dollars and up
2. Wedding dress alterations—$75–$100
3. Wedding cake—$200–$400
4. Wedding pictures—$500–$1,000
5. Videotape of the ceremony—$400
6. Wedding Reception—several thousand dollars

If these figures surprise you, be aware that I am giving you the conservative estimates!

But you don't need to be preparing for a wedding to be faced with decisions about how to spend your money. The panacea of material goodies in modern America is enough to make your head swim! Even an unbelievably adequate budget, by the standards of the world outside America, can become woefully inadequate by American standards, if we let it.

Part of the problem is that we think we need more than we do. You may remember the story about the young wife who told her husband, after a visit with the doctor, "Dear, the doctor said I am in a very distraught condition, and it is essential for me to go to St. Tropez, then to Aspen, and then buy myself a new mink wrap."

The husband immediately called the doctor: "What did you mean by all this stuff about St. Tropez, Aspen, and mink coats?"

46

The doctor replied, "I just recommended to your wife a regimen of frequent baths, plenty of fresh air, and to be sure to dress in warm clothes!"

Like that woman who wanted more than she needed, we often become dissatisfied with what we have and seek for more. I recently heard of a local bank that had put together a radio advertisement which aggressively marketed their home-improvement loans. The ad began by asking, "Are you dissatisfied with your home?" The spot continued, "Do you drive around other neighborhoods observing the fine homes, and then come home to note how bad your home looks in comparison?" Of course, that bank had the solution to your "problem." If you would just fill out a loan application, it would provide you with the money you "needed" to bring your home up to "acceptable" standards.

It seems to me there is a gross moral problem with ads of this nature, yet we are continually hounded by such messages. Each business tries to make us dissatisfied with what we have and strives to show us why we must purchase its particular product. Often these marketing techniques are detrimental to our income, especially when we, as Christians, are trying to sort out our priorities and set up a workable family budget!

SECRETS OF SATISFACTION

How can we counter the problem of wanting more than we need? How can we begin to set forth a budget that emphasizes Christian convictions?

In setting up a family budget which promotes Christian values and yet assures practicality in our society, we must acknowledge that *our level of satisfaction must be analyzed frequently.* Money of itself is neither good nor bad, but the way we spend it reflects who we are. It represents us in a practical form. By our spending choices, we can be either wise or foolish; we can further the kingdom of God, or we can indulge our selfishness. We can achieve the goals and priorities we have set for our lives, or we can satisfy our own selfish appetites.

The apostle Paul gives us one of the best examples for keeping our values in focus and receiving satisfaction from ministry, rather than from material goods. In his letter to the church at Philippi, he describes his secrets of satisfaction:

> Not that I complain of want; for I have learned, in whatever state I am, to be content. I know how to be abased, and I know how to abound; in any and all circumstances I have learned the secret of facing plenty and hunger, abundance and want. I can do all things in him who strengthens me. (4:11-13)

We too must begin to evaluate our life's purpose and cultivate attitudes of satisfaction. Then we are ready to begin setting up our family budgets within a Christian framework.

Let's put some figures to the drawing board!

MANAGING MONEY: THE GREAT CHALLENGE

No two families are alike. However, most personal-finance experts agree upon several general steps in setting up a workable family budget.[1]

Step 1. Establish a budget period. Most people set the period to correspond with the frequency of their paycheck. For example, if you are paid once a month, establish a monthly budget period.

Step 2. Sort expenditures into 4 categories.
  1. Fixed Monthly Expenses—items which occur each month as a fixed amount (i.e., rent, loans, tithe and contributions, savings)
  2. Variable Monthly Expenses—items which occur each

month, but amount varies (i.e., food, utilities, clothing, medical fees)
3. Fixed Infrequent Expenses—predictable items which occur 1–4 times per year (i.e., insurance, taxes, tuition)
4. Variable Infrequent Expenses—unpredictable items which occur only once a year or so (i.e., Christmas, vacations, "luxuries")

Step 3. Determine your annual income and divide it by 12.

Step 4. Compare expenditures to income. If your expenditures exceed income, you will need to trim a little fat off certain items. Start by reducing or eliminating your debt, which will lower the amount you pay in interest. Reevaluate your expectation and satisfaction levels. If there is no way to trim an already lean budget, consider ways to boost current family income by changing jobs or adding additional jobs. If you have more income than expenditures, thank the Lord and increase your areas of giving and saving.

Step 5. Revise your budget every six months or every year.

GETTING STARTED

A recent *U. S. News and World Report* article stated that 50 percent of all persons seeking a divorce list financial problems as the number-one problem.[2] If providing solutions to monetary problems is so important in maintaining family relationships, and if setting up a spending plan, or budget, helps to provide these solutions, it will be wise to *follow the budget we've set up for ourselves and our families.* But implementing the budget we have designed may not be easy! How can we be successful in sticking to our budget?

First of all, involve everyone in your family in the budgeting process. Have a family pow-wow to get input from each family member on how they would like to set up and carry out the new spending plan. Be sure all family members understand why a budget is important and what they can gain from following it. Even young children can contribute ideas about what to prioritize, ways to save, where to shop, and so on. My eight-year-old granddaughter loves to shop at a budget grocery store because she gets to sack her own groceries!

Second, sticking to your budget will be more successful if more than one family member participates in record keeping and bill paying. If one member dislikes bill paying, take turns, or give that person a different but related job. In our family, I have always handled most of the bill paying because I enjoy seeing how far I can stretch the dollars. My wife reciprocates by helping with record keeping and by making sure the desk I use is cleaned off! Every family is different, but no matter how you assign specific tasks, each member should be conscious of how the family money is being spent, and how well that spending pattern reflects the predetermined budget.

Third, allow a little flexibility in your budget. Children, as well as adults, enjoy a personal allowance for lunches, cosmetics, entertainment, and small miscellaneous items. When each penny is scrutinized to the extreme, life can become sheer drudgery. Just be sure to allow for these extras in your budget. A miscellaneous category could include personal allowances, as well as unavoidable but unplanned expenditures.

Here are some additional tips I feel are important for responsible and successful money management:

1. *Expenditures should be made jointly.* Discuss purchases and agree to buy them as a family. This helps to eliminate arguments, because no one person gets all the blame if a purchase doesn't work out. This acts as a good check-and-balance system. Many times I may consider buying an item, but after Ann and I discuss it together, we decide to wait or not make the purchase at all.

2. *Don't buy what you can't afford.* When you borrow, you pay interest, so this means you should avoid debt whenever possible. A $10,000 car becomes a $13,000 expense when you add on the interest, so consider whether you want to pay $13,000 for a $10,000 car. Many of us think we have no choice but to make monthly car payments. Often that may be true, but first consider driving a current car longer or purchasing a less expensive car.

3. *Avoid get-rich-quick schemes;* there are few shortcuts in life.

SAVING FOR A RAINY DAY

A good rule of thumb is to save approximately 15 percent of your income for a future day. Divide the money you save into two accounts. First, establish an Emergency Fund of easily retrievable money which contains enough income for one to two months. This is the "rainy day" money set aside for major unexpected expenditures. Second, create a Long-range Account, into which you slowly put aside up to three months' salary in low-risk savings. Once these accounts are established, you can begin to earmark money for larger household purchases and other needs, such as college, travel, retirement, and so on. Churches and other worthy organizations can advise you of ways to save your money, while helping someone else in the process. Get at it!

IS THERE ANYTHING LEFT TO GIVE?

If the only information someone had about you came from your checkbooks for the last five years, what would they know about your life? About your character? About your priorities? I heard a story about a candidate for the Communist party who was undergoing an examination.

"Comrade," he was asked, "what would you do if you were left two million rubles?"

"I would give one million to the party and keep the other million for myself," he answered.

"Very good. And if you had two houses?"

"I would give one to the party and keep the other for myself."

"Excellent. Now tell me what you would do if you had two pair of trousers?"

There was a long pause, and then the candidate said weakly, "Comrade, I don't know."

"Why not?"

"Well, you see, I *have* two pair of trousers."

Sound familiar? Often we support giving as long as someone else is giving; we promote benevolence as long as someone else is generous. But when it begins to hit our own pocketbook, we're not sure if we can, or even want to, make the sacrifices necessary.

The Bible tells many stories of those who wanted to give, but on their own terms. The tragic story of Cain and Abel teaches us a serious lesson: *God wants our first fruits—gifts of priority and sacrifice.*

The Old Testament detailed God's terms for giving; the concept of tithing was basic. Leviticus 27:30-32 discusses the amount to be set aside for the Lord as a minimum:

> All the tithe of the land, whether of the seed of the land or of the fruit of the trees, is the LORD's; it is holy to the LORD. If a man wishes to redeem any of his tithe, he shall add a fifth to it. And all the tithe of herds and flocks, every tenth animal of all that pass under the herdsman's staff, shall be holy to the LORD.

The New Testament expands the idea of tithing through the larger concept of stewardship. Stewardship means that we use responsibly every resource that God places in our hands—that is, we use every resource for the glory of God and the good of humankind. Stewardship demands that we put first things first in our lives. It forces us to choose to Whom our allegiance will be. Jesus reminded his followers:

> Do not lay up for yourselves treasures on earth, where moth and rust consume and where thieves break in and steal, but lay up for yourselves treasures in heaven, where neither moth nor rust consumes and where thieves do not break in and steal. For where your treasure is, there will your heart be also. (Matt. 6:19-21)

> No one can serve two masters; for either he will hate the one and love the other, or he will be devoted to the one and despise the other. You cannot serve God and mammon. (Matt. 6:24)

John Wesley, the founder of Methodism, said,

> By whatever means thy riches increase, whether with or without labor, whether by trade, legacies, or any other way, unless your charities increase in the same proportion, unless thou givest a full tenth of the substance of thy fixed and occasional income, thou dost undoubtedly set thy heart upon thy gold and it shall eat thy flesh as fire.[3]

Our real basis for giving is encapsulated in First Chronicles 29:14 of *The Living Bible:* "Everything we have has come from you, and we only give you what is yours already!" Everything we have belongs to God, and we only give back 10 percent.

Our minimum standard today as Christians begins with the tithe. The top 10 percent belongs to God. This is God's money. Ten percent may seem like a considerable amount to some. However, it is the minimum biblical standard of giving. If you plan to be serious about living your life as a disciple of the Lord Jesus Christ, you won't hesitate to tithe. The world will not change until we begin the process of sacrifice and self-denial in our own lives by our examples of giving. A better world will never be cheaply achieved.

In my opinion, a tithe belongs to the local church. It belongs to the place where you have taken your vow to follow Jesus Christ. In the local church, you should be a participant in how that money is spent. You will not always have your way—as a pastor, I surely do not. But I have the right and the responsibility to help build the kingdom of God in the lives of believers in the church. Any amount I give beyond the 10 percent can go to other worthy causes to which I feel the Lord would have me contribute.

SECOND-MILE GIVING

I recently heard a story which challenged me to a spirit of true giving. It's about a boy named Billy and a Christmas pageant that went awry.

Billy was eight years old that year, and quite big to be in second grade. Still, he was well-liked by the other children in his class. He was a helpful boy, willing and smiling, and a natural protector of the underdog. When the older boys chased the younger ones away, it was always Billy who said, "Can't they stay? They're no bother."

Billy fancied the idea of being a shepherd with a flute in the Christmas pageant that year, but the play's director assigned him a more important role. The innkeeper did not have many lines, and Billy's size would make his refusal of lodging to Joseph more forceful.

The usual large audience gathered for the town's yearly extravaganza. Billy stood in the wings, watching with fascination.

Then Joseph appeared—slowly, tenderly guiding Mary—and knocked hard on the wooden door set into the painted backdrop.

"What do you want?" Billy the innkeeper said brusquely, swinging the door open.

"We seek lodging," Joseph answered.

54

"Seek it elsewhere." Billy looked straight ahead but spoke vigorously. "The inn is filled."

"Sir, we have asked everywhere in vain. We have traveled far and are weary."

"There is no room in this inn for you." Billy looked properly stern.

"Please, good innkeeper, this is my wife, Mary. She is heavy with child. Surely you must have some small corner for her to rest."

Now, for the first time, the innkeeper looked down at Mary. There was a long pause, long enough to make the audience tense with embarrassment.

"No! Be gone!" the prompter whispered from the wings.

"No!" Billy repeated. "Be gone!"

Joseph sadly placed his arm around Mary. Mary lay her head upon her husband's shoulder, and the two of them started to move away. Billy stood in the doorway, watching the forlorn couple. His mouth was open, his brow creased with concern, his eyes filling unmistakably with tears.

And suddenly this Christmas pageant became different from all others.

"Don't go, Joseph," Billy called out. "Bring Mary back." He broke out in a bright smile. "You can have my room!"

A few people thought the pageant had been ruined because Billy had spontaneously changed the lines. Most considered it the best Christmas pageant they had ever seen. Billy had spoken in the true Christmas spirit.

This is stewardship in its finest sense: the second-mile giving to God of ourselves and our possessions, without restraint—to use for God's glory, with no strings attached.

WHERE DO I GO FROM HERE?

Money is here to stay! It is an important part of our lives. We have no choice but to deal with money exchange if we live in an organized society.

But we can choose whether *we* want to control our money, or whether we let *it* control us. We can make responsible choices as Christians in spending our money. We can choose to be satisfied with less instead of more. We can set up workable budgets to hold the reigns on our spending patterns. We can prioritize our habits so that giving and saving are a part of our everyday living. And in so doing, we "serve God instead of mammon."

JOURNAL JOTS

For Fun: If I suddenly inherited $100,000, how would I spend the money? _____

_____

_____

For Discovery: Read as many passages about giving patterns as you can find. For starters, see Genesis 14:20, 28:22; Deuteronomy 14:22-23, 28-29; Proverbs 3:9-10; Malachi 3:7-10; Mark 10:17-22; Luke 6:30-31; Acts 2:43-47; II Corinthians 9:6-15; I Timothy 6:6-10. Use a concordance to find even more passages. List the main ideas in those passages.

1. _____

2. _____

3. _____

4. _____

5. _____

How can unselfish giving patterns contribute to a healthy personal budget? _____

_____

_____

For Commitment This Week: I will set up a workable budget for my family and, with God's help, use it as a tool to reorder my life.

C H A P T E R
IV

The Lion of
Family Relationships
Protecting an Endangered Species

PERSONAL INVENTORY: How well do you know your
family?

Complete the following statements with the answer you think is
most accurate. (Skip questions that do not apply to your family
situation.) Then check your responses by asking the appropriate
family members the questions that pertain to them. How many
answers did you predict correctly? Give yourself 10 points for
each reasonably correct answer; 5 points for somewhat similar
answers! If your score is 40 or above, pat yourself on the back!
Between 20 and 40, you have no cause to brag, but you
apparently possess moderate communication skills. If you scored
20 or less, you'd better take a crash course in communication!

1. My spouse's favorite place for a night out:

2. My son or daughter's favorite teacher:

3. My son or daughter's least favorite teacher:

4. My son or daughter's favorite toy:

5. My mother's favorite meal:

6. My father's favorite hobby:

7. My grandmother's favorite childhood memory:

8. My grandfather's proudest moment:

DO ONLY THE STRONGEST SURVIVE?

How can a Christian family survive in today's world? And not only how can a Christian family survive, but how can the members enjoy one another's company and move toward fulfilling God's purpose for them on earth? How can we keep the family unit intact in the midst of a segmented society?

One of the biggest problems in today's families is that we don't have time for one another. Years ago my youngest daughter overheard me telling someone that the average middle-class father spends 37 seconds per day with his small child.

Soon afterward, she entered my study and announced, "I need my 37 seconds now!"

Somehow we expect to *have* family relationships without budgeting the *time* to build those relationships. Somehow we expect to maintain a close family without taking the time to communicate to one another our needs, hopes, and dreams. Keeping the family unit intact takes commitment. And commitment takes *time*.

When Dr. Alan McGinnis, an accomplished marriage counselor and family therapist, was asked what he thought caused the breakup of so many marriages, he answered, "I think most marriages die of neglect. Pure and simple neglect."[1]

Communication between family members cannot happen in a few short minutes during the day, or in the wee hours of the morning. *If we want to successfully build special relationships with our family, we must be willing to pay the price of time*—minutes and hours and weeks and months and years—spent getting to know, love, and respect one another. We must become a part of one another's experiences.

Our neglect of family relationships reminds me of the woman who appeared in court to obtain a divorce.

After some questioning, the judge said to her, "I have been listening for some time to your testimony about your husband, and it seems to me that you have only a small complaint. Are you seriously trying to obtain a divorce on the grounds that your husband has been careless about his appearance?"

The woman answered, "Yes, your Honor; he hasn't appeared for over a year!"

PRIORITIES . . . AGAIN?

Go back to chapter 1 and reexamine the priorities you set for yourself. Reevaluate the way you spend your time with your family. We all have twenty-four hours in a day. The big question is, How will we choose to spend that time?

It is important to consciously budget get-to-know-one-another time if you want to build family relationships. Set aside thirty minutes to an hour a day, just to relax and catch up on what has happened with the family members during the day. Watch out for the invasion of television upon your family time. You can't improve communication between family members when all eyes and ears are focused on the TV set. If your career takes you out of town often, you will need to find blocks of time on the days you *are* home. Don't be afraid to close your mouth and listen to what your family has to say! In my family, we often do our communicating late at night! At least at that hour, we can minimize interruptions such as the telephone!

Don't hesitate to talk often about your faith and moral philosophies. (I've always been good at this one!) I used to preach to my girls about the evils of smoking and drinking. One summer we vacationed in Kentucky, and as we drove through the countryside, I noticed a rotting tobacco leaf by the side of the road. I stopped the car, got out, picked it up, and reminded the girls that even pigs would not eat these leaves. When I held it in front of my girls' noses, they shrieked in disgust. Needless to say, my girls never have, and I'm certain never will, smoke!

Set aside time each day for family prayer and Bible reading. I will give my wife much credit in this area. Through the years as our children were growing up, she would gather the family for devotions. Many nights I would arrive home from a meeting at the church and hear her reading a Bible story to one of our girls. She quoted Bible verses and sang hymns so frequently that each daughter has a backlog of verses and Christian songs stored in her memory, ready to be brought to mind when needed.

> You shall therefore lay up these words of mine in your heart and in your soul; and you shall bind them as a sign upon your hand, and they shall be as frontlets between your eyes. And you shall teach them to your children, talking of them when you are sitting in your house, and when you are walking by the way, and when you lie down, and when you rise. And you shall write them upon the doorposts of your house and upon your gates. (Deut. 11:18-20)

Finally, use the time you set aside for your family to show interest in your spouse's work and your children's activities. Once a week, attend an activity or share a hobby with each member. Spend one-on-one time with your spouse and each of your children as often as possible. Take walks or ride bikes together. Have picnics or eat out. Spend moments reading or telling stories to your children. Let there be talk time. Time is a treasure in itself, and it goes so fast! Don't let your children grow up without getting to know them. Don't lose touch with your spouse. Make every moment count!

BEING REAL

In Margery Williams' magical tale of *The Velveteen Rabbit*, the wise old experienced Skin Horse tries to explain to the Velveteen Rabbit about being "real":

"What is REAL?" asked the Rabbit one day. "Does it mean having things that buzz inside of you and a stick-out handle?" "Real isn't how you are made," said the Skin Horse. "It's a thing that happens to you. When a child loves you for a long, long time, not just to play with, but REALLY loves you, then you become Real."

"Does it hurt?"

"Well, sometimes," said the Skin Horse, for he was always truthful. "But when you are Real you don't mind being hurt."

"Does it happen all at once, like being wound up, or is it bit by bit?"

"It doesn't happen all at once," said the Skin Horse. "You become. It takes a long time. That's why it doesn't often happen to people who break easily, or who have sharp edges, or who have to be carefully kept. Generally, by the time you are Real, most of your hair has been loved off, and your eyes drop out, and you get loose in the joints and very shabby. But these things don't matter much at all, because once you are Real, you can't be ugly, except to people who don't understand."[2]

One of the best ways I know to build family relationships is to *foster the development of intimacy between family members.* Learn to be "real" with each other! The family is the only place, outside of the church, where persons can find unconditional love and acceptance. The family can provide a haven of intimacy *with no strings attached.* Within the enclave of the family, we can be ourselves, loved and accepted, just for who we are.

Intimacy, like communication, doesn't just happen. How can a family develop close relationships? I have found that one way to build intimacy is through physical expressions of love. Hugs, love pats, hand-holding—these are special graces a family can share. For example, my wife loves to sit on my lap! And I love for her to do it! All the cares and burdens of the day seem to pale when I say, "Come here, honey, and sit on my lap!" I can give her my undivided attention, we share our vulnerabilities with each other, and she feels loved in an extraordinary, un-threatening way.

The words we say to our family members can offer reassurances of our love. When my middle daughter read this chapter, she commented, "I remember, Dad, how you said—more times than I could count—'I'm for you!'" How powerful those three words are! When I spoke them, I wanted my daughter to know that I supported her, trusted her, and cared about her unconditionally. My love for her had no strings attached.

Dr. James C. Dobson discusses yet another way to build intimacy. He emphasizes the need for positive interactions between a parent and child at a time when the parent is not demanding anything of the child. He quotes from Dr. Fitzhugh Dodson's *How to Father:*

> Analyze how your child sees you: Is 99 percent of your role one in which you are expecting something of him, reminding him to do something, scolding him to stop doing something, or getting after him for misbehaving? If so, you are not building a deep positive emotional relationship. He needs time with you when you are not demanding anything from him, time when the two of you are mutually enjoying yourselves.[3]

Even God said, "I AM WHO I AM" (Exod. 3:14). God did not choose to justify, defend, or characterize himself. God is who God is—no more, no less. That is all the explanation that is given to the people.

Jesus gave his life to demonstrate true, unselfish love. He developed relationships throughout his ministry, taking people from every phase of life and loving them just as they were. Consider his disciples, the woman caught in adultery, the woman with an issue of blood, the rich young ruler. Jesus gave each of them an opportunity, through his love and acceptance, to develop an intimate relationship with him.

What a responsibility we have been given in our family relationships! We can choose to establish nonthreatening, intimate relationships with our children, our spouse, our parents—any family member. We all need huge doses of unconditional love. Often we are cut down at every point by others in the world, but in the family we can build self-esteem through caring relationships. In so doing, our love for one another mirrors the love of God in our world.

Work at making your family relationships free from critical attitudes and responses, and full of unconditional love and acceptance. Reach out and touch! Bite your tongue if you have to, count to ten if necessary, and soon you will find negative habits of criticism giving way to positive practices of praise. Intimacy will make its way into your home!

HISTORY AND TRADITIONS—WHO NEEDS THEM?

I've always been fascinated with history. I guess I inherited that love from my mother. As a child, I would sit and listen while she read to me from her history books. She loved to quote "history"! Then at seminary, I decided to major in church history.

On our honeymoon, we visited many spots that held our ancestral roots as we made our way through the southern states. And when the girls were young, we made a special trip to Minnesota just so they could see their grandfather's birthplace. For years, we traveled to Oklahoma City to spend Thanksgiving with the Morell family. In more recent times, I have made special efforts to keep close ties with my grandchildren, though they live some distance away.

There is something about history and traditions that warms my heart. I love to perpetuate the old. It brings stability, centralness, and identity to my life. It helps me discover who I am. I like knowing that our family has been, and always will be, in church on Sunday morning. I like celebrating the special holidays of Christmas and Easter. And I think my family feels the same.

Keeping old traditions and memories alive is paramount to

64

family-building. One of our most memorable family traditions takes place once a year. Every Christmas Eve, for as long as I can remember, each of us has opened one present. As a child, it was exciting for me to be allowed to open one present "early." As a parent and later a grandparent, I have enjoyed watching the children closest to me experience that pleasure. But always, in the midst of the excitement of giving and receiving gifts, I tell the story so that all can remember the reason we open one gift on Christmas Eve.

When my mother was a young newlywed—living in Oklahoma City, some thousand miles from her Georgia roots—her father lay critically ill on Christmas Eve. I'm sure she felt very homesick and most anxious to be by his side in Georgia, but it was not possible to make the expensive journey. Not fully knowing his condition and uncertain as to what the coming days would bring, Mom and Dad each opened a single gift, with the hope that her dad's health might begin to return in the coming hours. Disappointingly, Christmas morning brought the news of his death. Thus, in remembrance of "Sweet Papa," and to remind us to make the most of the gift of each day our Lord gives us, every Christmas Eve each member of the Morell family has opened one gift. It's a not-to-be-forgotten tradition.

Perpetuating old traditions unifies a family through sharing unique experiences. And creating new traditions accomplishes the same binding purpose. New traditions allow every family member a hand in memory-making.

One of the fun things about having grandchildren is that you can establish new traditions with them. Last year I had the opportunity to take my oldest grandson with me to the Holy Land. We had a grand time! But his younger sister was quick to inform me that she couldn't wait until she was old enough to go on a trip with me. Knowing her, she won't let me off the hook! Like it or not, I had established a new tradition: The Lord willing, I plan to take each of my grandchildren on a trip as soon as they are old enough. Right now, they are eagerly waiting in line! What a family-builder this new tradition already has been! I reap the benefit of really getting to know my grandchildren one-on-one, they get to know me, *and* we get a trip out of it, too!

Think about the last time you established a new tradition. Maybe it was going out for ice cream after the annual piano recital, or going Christmas caroling in your neighborhood. Maybe it was attending an Easter sunrise service, baking cookies for the last day of school, or traveling on a yearly family vacation.

Maybe you haven't started a new tradition recently! Why not ask all the members of the family to think of a new tradition they would like to initiate? Starting new traditions has been so meaningful in my family, I hope you will want to share in the joy! Family relationships and love are built in the process!

LOVE MEANS NEVER HAVING TO SAY YOU'RE SORRY?

A number of years ago the movie *Love Story* made its way to the screen. One of the climactic lines was spoken by the heroine, who was dying of cancer. Her hero had just acted insensitively toward her, and as he attempted to apologize, she interrupted him with the statement which since has been heard around the world with mixed reviews: "Love means never having to say you're sorry."

That attitude has set many perfectionists on the road to misery, many egotists on the way to greater obnoxiousness, many marriages on the rocks, and many children to the doctor with ulcers. For you see, when the role of forgiveness in family relationships is ignored, chaos is sure to follow.

Forgiveness provides the cement to positive family relationships. The idea that one never needs to admit to being sorry in love relationships is fatalistic. On the contrary, true love relationships should exercise the words "I'm sorry" in abundance.

Teach your children the importance of saying "I'm sorry" and

66

"I was wrong." As they become older, this attitude of taking responsibility for their wrongdoings will be part of their life-style.

Jesus emphasized forgiveness in his ministry. God's purpose in sending Jesus to earth was to reconcile us to God. God knew that because of our human nature we would make many mistakes, but we were given a second chance through forgiveness. Through Christ's death on the cross, we can have a new life free from guilt and sin, just for the asking.

Not only do we receive forgiveness with God through Christ, but we pass on that forgiveness to others. The first part of the statement, "And forgive us our debts," is not complete without the second part: "As we also have forgiven our debtors" (Matt. 6:12). In fact, whether we can be restored to a right relationship with God seems maddeningly dependent upon whether we first reconcile ourselves to our brothers and sisters. Jesus put it this way:

> Therefore, if you are offering your gift at the altar and there remember that your brother has something against you, leave your gift there in front of the altar. First go and be reconciled to your brother; then come and offer your gift. (Matt. 5:23-24 NIV)

How important it is for us to pass on these principles of forgiveness within the relationships of our families! We should not expect perfection in our dealings with one another. We need to recognize that from time to time we will make errors in judgment, speak thoughtless words, act insensitively. We will make mistakes in our attitudes and actions, and it will be necessary to genuinely confess our shortcomings and ask for forgiveness. Then we can go to God in repentance, and God will give us renewed strength to strive for better ways.

I remember all too well the time I almost irreparably severed my relationship with my teenage daughter. When she was in the ninth grade, she belonged to a girls' drill team. The girls practiced every day after school during football season, working on their routines for the upcoming game. One day when I went to pick her up, the team continued to practice well beyond the announced time. The next day it happened again. By the third day of delayed departure, I began to fume. Why, I was busy! How inconsiderate the teacher was of my time and that of the other parents! We couldn't just wait indefinitely! So I appointed myself spokesman for the group and headed for the gym where the girls were practicing. Much to my daughter's dismay, I rather loudly told the teacher how I felt about her lack of consideration and inability to stick to a schedule, and then removed my daughter. Of course, my daughter was humiliated! Mortified! Totally devastated! She never wanted to show her face at school again! In fact, though my daughter is now an adult, she still remembers that occurrence with less than positive emotions!

Was I wrong? I don't think so. Was the teacher inconsiderate? Of course! Nevertheless, I had failed to realize the impact that my actions—though justified—would have on the all-too-fragile psyche of my teenage daughter. I had to beg forgiveness, even though I wasn't quite sure why I was so cornered. I had caused one of the single most embarrassing moments in her life, and I would have been an insensitive clod, had I not recognized my precarious situation and tried to rectify the consequences of my actions.

Make forgiveness a way of life! Provide allowances for one another's decisions and mistakes. Help the family to be a place where each member feels loved and accepted in spite of her or his actions. In this atmosphere of unconditional love and acceptance, family members can offer to one another, and to the world, a flicker of what agape love is all about.

THE FIRST PARENT HAD TROUBLE TOO.

The immortal Bill Cosby tells a tongue-in-cheek story about the perils of parenting:

After creating the heaven, the earth, the oceans, and the entire animal kingdom, God created Adam and Eve. And the first thing He said to them was "Don't." To the animals, He never said, "Don't"—He hurled no negatives at the elephant—but to the brightest of His creatures, the ones who get into Yale, He said, "Don't."

"Don't what?" Adam replied.

"Don't eat the forbidden fruit."

"Forbidden fruit? Really? Where is it?"

Is this beginning to sound familiar? . . .

"It's over there," said God, wondering why He hadn't stopped after making the elephants.

A few minutes later, God saw the kids having an apple break and He was angry.

"Didn't I *tell* you not to eat that fruit?" the First Parent said.

"Uh-huh," Adam replied.

"Then why *did* you?"

"I don't know," Adam said.

At least he didn't say, "No problem."

"All right then, get out of here! Go forth, become fruitful, and multiply!"

This was not a blessing but a curse: God's punishment was that Adam and Eve should have children of their own . . . a couple of dim-witted boys. One of these boys couldn't stand the other; but instead of just leaving Eden and going to Chicago, he had to kill him.

Thus the pattern was set and it never has changed. But there is reassurance in this story for those of you whose children are not doing well. . . . If *God* had trouble handling children, what makes you think it would be a piece of cake for you?[4]

Building strong family relationships is not easy! You must budget your time so that communication can occur, find ways of making your family unique through establishing and following traditions, and realize that you will make some mistakes in the process. However, the rewards of enjoying one another's company and having a good time sharing life together can make all your efforts worthwhile.

JOURNAL JOTS

Have every family member who is old enough set aside one hour this week to sit down together and discuss the following questions. Let one member read the questions, and give each member an opportunity to answer.

For Fun:
1. If you were given an all-expenses-paid vacation for your family, would you:
    a. Cash it in?
    b. Give it to your worst enemy?
    c. Celebrate by leaving a day early?

2. If you could choose any place in the world to take your vacation, where would you go? _____

For Discovery: God meant for families to celebrate life together. What secrets do the following passages of Scripture offer your family?

1. Deuteronomy 6:4-9
2. Psalm 127
3. Proverbs 3:5-6
4. Matthew 5:23-24
5. Matthew 6:25-34
6. Philippians 4:4-8

_____

_____

_____

For Commitment This Week: I will set aside a short but uninterrupted time each day for family-building.

C H A P T E R
V

The Lion of Depression
Sometimes I Don't Want to Get Up in the Morning!

PERSONAL INVENTORY: Are my feelings really that important?

Check the following that apply:

1. When I am depressed, I:

_____ cry.   feel sorry   _____ pray.

_____ eat too much.   _____ for myself.   _____ read Scripture.

_____ gripe a lot.   _____ become angry.   _____ listen to music.

withdraw from   wonder if   _____ take a walk.

_____ the world.   _____ God cares.   don't let

_____ anyone know.

2. When I sense that a friend or family member is depressed, I:

_____ ask what is wrong.   _____ try to cheer him/her up.

_____ say nothing.   _____ pray for him/her.

_____ sympathize.   _____ chastise him/her.

_____ empathize.

3. On the line below, place a dot to indicate how important you would rate the problem of depression in your life at this time.

_____

very much a problem   not a problem

71

DEPRESSION—WHO, ME?

In the comic strip *Peanuts,* one of the episodes features Charlie Brown and his friend Lucy as they take a cruise on the "sea of life."

Lucy asks Charlie Brown: "When we sit on this ship of life in our deck chairs, do we face toward the front, or the back?"

Charlie replies typically: "Lucy, I haven't even figured out how to open these things yet!"

This anecdote aptly summarizes many of our feelings about life. We are reluctant even to admit that Christians can suffer from depression, much less discuss the subject to find ways we can begin to cope. Most of us have no idea what to do about depression when it strikes our lives, and certainly we can offer little help or hope to others as they struggle. We are still trying to get life working right for us—we are still trying to get the deck chairs unfolded. All of us, at one time or another, suffer from feelings of failure, inadequacy, depression. Let's face it—circumstances and physical ailments do affect our sense of well-being. Mild depression and moderate mood swings are a part of being confined to our human body, with its human emotions. How can we help ourselves when we suffer from depression? What can we do to help others when they are depressed? The good news is that there is hope and help for the depressed Christian!

WHAT'S WRONG WITH ME?

Exactly what *is* depression? Webster's defines *depress* as "to load a person or thing so heavily that he or it sinks under the weight. *Depress* now chiefly implies a lowering of spirits, of activity, or the like, by mental or physical [or spiritual] causes."

What can you do if you suffer from depression? How can you

help someone who suffers from depression? First of all, I would suggest that you start your treatment with a physical checkup. (Often, an endocrinologist is a good place to start. You may need to seek a second opinion if you get no help the first time around.) *If your depression stems from a physical problem, you must get to the root of it before your depression will improve.* Medical researchers learn more every day about how physical changes in one's body can cause, or at least worsen, symptoms of depression.

What physical changes can contribute to depression? Apparently, doctors and scientists are just beginning to touch the tip of the iceberg. An article titled "The Medical and Biological Effects of Light" discusses the problems of Seasonal Affective Disorder (SAD)—depressive episodes related to the seasonal variations. Certain people are especially sensitive to the shorter days of winter, which bring with them less exposure to light rays. A cluster of symptoms, including fatigue, sadness, hypersomnia, overeating, carbohydrate craving, and weight gain, characterize a person with SAD. Medical researchers have reversed these symptoms by exposing sensitive persons to additional hours of light.[1]

Menopause, with its accompanying hormone imbalances, can cause depression. Often restoring the proper, God-given chemical balance through adding hormones or supplying medication can relieve, if not eliminate, depression. Dr. James C. Dobson, in his booklet *Understanding Menopause*, tells about the unrelenting depression his mother experienced for weeks at a time, as a result of hormone deficiencies. A physician, a long-time friend of the Dobson family, found the problem:

[She was] in a state of extreme estrogen deprival as a consequence of menopause, and he prescribed an immediate injection of this essential hormone. She returned a week later for a second injection, and continued every seven days for years to come. Though her "cure" did not occur instantaneously, the effect of the medication was like turning from darkness to light. Her depression vanished . . . she became interested in life again and the woman we had known and loved through the years was with us once more.[2]

Other physical problems can directly or indirectly cause depression. Major surgery, ovarian dysfunction, endocrine imbalance, and a host of other diseases can affect one's emotional system. Even minor illnesses can temporarily weaken the immune system and make one more susceptible to depression. How important it is to take care of one's body by receiving proper medical care, the needed amounts of sleep, and good nutrition! The good Lord has intricately woven our emotions into our physical bodies. Don't ignore physical problems as a source of depression.

MAYBE IT ISN'T AS BAD AS IT SEEMS.

Many times our mental attitudes lead us into depression. I had an experience recently which shows how easy it is to become depressed because of circumstances that do not even exist. My wife and I have a close friend whose mother was in the hospital awaiting surgery. I made my way quickly to the Intensive Care Unit and a nurse showed me to Virginia's room. I prayed for her fervently because she appeared to be much worse than I had expected.

As I left the hospital, I met our friend Juanita and commented that her mother did not seem to be doing too well. My words concerned Juanita. She raced to her mother's room and began to quiz her about my visit, but her mother could remember nothing about my being there. All day, family members kept trying to jog her memory, but finally, Virginia's loved ones felt their worst fears were confirmed: Virginia was indeed quite ill.

After some detective work, it was determined that there were two Virginia Parkers in the hospital. I had prayed for the wrong one! Juanita's Virginia sailed through the subsequent surgery, once she knew that senility had not yet set in! The other Virginia must have told friends on earth or in heaven that an angel had visited her.

TRY TO THINK OPTIMISTICALLY!

Circumstances sometimes are not as bad as they seem. But even when times are genuinely difficult, we need to learn how to cultivate habits of scriptural thinking. Here is what Paul told the church at Philippi:

> Finally, brethren, whatever is true, whatever is honorable, whatever is just, whatever is pure, whatever is lovely, whatever is gracious, if there is any excellence, if there is anything worthy of praise, think about these things. (Phil. 4:8)

How can we cultivate positive thoughts? How can we develop new attitudes? Often we are not capable of changing our heart by an act of our will. But by the continual act of our will to invite the Holy Spirit to do that work of transformation in us, we can contribute substantially to the changing of our attitudes.

Even in the midst of our depression, we can find things for which to be thankful. There is a story about one optimistic minister who, in his opening prayer each Sunday, always thanked God for the weather. On a particularly cold, icy, windy, slushy Sunday morning, the few people who had ventured out wondered how the minister could possibly refer to that day's weather with any sense of gratitude. To their surprise, he began his prayer: "Dear God, we thank thee that thou dost send us so few Sundays like today."

We can thank God for the positive circumstances in our lives, however small. We can thank God for the character-building we receive when we suffer. We can even thank God for the sensitivity and compassion we learn and experience in the midst of our depression.

Paul and Silas learned the secret of being thankful in all things. When they were imprisoned in Philippi, despite being beaten and put into stocks, at midnight they began to sing praises to God. Even the other prisoners were listening to them! (Acts 16:11-40).

How many of us can remain that positive in the midst of such negative circumstances? How did Paul and Silas do it? What secret did they know that would be of help to us? They knew that *God was in control,* even while they were in jail. They were quite sure that the Lord was with them, whether they were preaching on the street or behind bars. By singing praises, by focusing their thoughts on God—an ever-present help—they were able to keep an attitude of gratitude in a very negative situation.

Many other passages of Scripture can give us positive attitudes upon which to focus:

The joy of the LORD is your strength. (Neh. 8:10c)

A glad heart makes a cheerful countenance,
but by sorrow of heart the spirit is broken. (Prov. 15:13)

We are afflicted in every way, but not crushed;
Perplexed, but not driven to despair;
Persecuted, but not forsaken;
Struck down, but not destroyed;
Always carrying in the body the death of Jesus,
so that the life of Jesus may also be manifested in our
bodies. (II Cor. 4:8-10)

So we do not lose heart. Though our outer nature is wasting away, our inner nature is being renewed every day. For this slight momentary affliction is preparing for us an eternal weight of glory beyond all comparison, because we look not to the things that are seen but to the things that are unseen; for the things that are seen are transient, but the things that are unseen are eternal. (II Cor. 4:16-18)

EXPECTATIONS AND EXCUSES

Not only do we need to develop new attitudes, *we also need to get our expectations right.* Too many foolish expectations can cause depression. We should not expect perfection in our relationships, or from ourselves.

What kinds of ridiculous expectations do we set for ourselves? Louis Harris, in his public opinion study *Inside America,* noted that two out of every three adults in the United States say they fidget, fuss, take furtive glances in windows and mirrors, and study other people's reactions to the way they look. Among this group, 94 percent of all men and 99 percent of all women said they would like to change something about their physical appearance.[3] Most people have set unrealistic expectations for their personal appearance; they have never learned to be happy with how they look. We somehow think we should look like the model in the magazine or the actor or actress on television. And invariably, we come up short. Our expectations cause us to feel unfulfilled.

Many times, our expectations for ourselves are so high that we continually make excuses for our shortcomings, instead of facing them squarely and still continuing to love ourselves. The following Alibi Chart for baseball gives a tongue-in-cheek example of this:

1. "I was looking for a fast ball." (after striking out)
2. "The sun got in my eyes." (dropped a fly ball)
3. "The ball slipped out of my hand." (wild throw)
4. "Two of the globes are out in that light out there." (line drive went by him for a triple)
5. "I got the uniforms mixed." (threw to wrong base)

Our expectations for marriage or career are often too high as well. We set our partner or our work experience up for failure by not allowing for human error. Because of our foolish expectations, we can't help feeling let down when things don't go just as we had planned, or when others don't perform just as we had hoped.

What can we do to help set more realistic expectations for ourselves and others, without using this as an excuse for mediocre behavior?

The Great Commandment and its sequel, the Golden Rule, offer the advice we need (Matt. 22:34-40; 7:12). If we can hold them as our standard of expectation, our lives will be more fulfilling, and we will experience disappointment less frequently. Setting our priorities to love God first, to love ourselves second, and to do and be to others what we wish they would do and be to us, can set scriptural expectations for our relationships with ourselves and others. If we will open ourselves so that we are a channel for forgiveness, instead of a yardstick for measuring the behavior of others, we will be happier and healthier in life.

I WANT TO BE LOVED BY YOU!

A depressed person needs a support person or group. If you are depressed, seek out at least one person with whom you can discuss your innermost feelings. You may find a listening ear in a family member, a close friend, or a person in your church. You also may want to talk with your pastor. You need to seek professional help from a Christian counselor if:

- Your everyday life becomes affected.
- Your depression doesn't lift—it remains chronic.
- You need a fresh outlook on an old problem.
- Your depression continues to rob you of the joy of the Christian life.
- You have recurring suicidal thoughts.

Do not be too proud or hesitant to talk with others about your problem. Paul reminded the Galatians to "bear one another's burdens, and so fulfill the law of Christ" (Gal. 6:2). By allowing others the chance to minister to you, you provide them with a special blessing. Help often is just around the corner, if you are not afraid to ask for it.

Not only should we ask for help when we need it, but we must be willing to be support persons for others, should the need arise. We don't need any major qualifications. Just a listening ear and a shoulder to cry on may be all the help someone needs.

Pastor Stephen Brown, in *When Your Rope Breaks*, tells about the first time he had to deal with a death in his congregation.

> I knew all the right things to say; I had been trained in dealing with grief; I was reasonably articulate. I prepared what I would say to the grieving wife, and as I drove to her house, I went over it in my mind.
>
> But when I got there, I lost it all. I tried to say some comforting things and made such a mess out of it that I just shut up and sat on the couch. It was one of the most miserable times in my ministry. When I drove away from the house, I was ashamed and humiliated. I was a pastor of a flock, yet this pastor had done nothing except sit and watch.
>
> After the funeral two or three days later, the widow came into my study. I started to apologize to her, but before I could speak she said, "Pastor, I want to thank you for all you have done for me. I don't know how I could have gotten through this without you."
>
> I couldn't believe my ears. "But," I said, "I didn't do anything."
>
> I'll never forget that woman's statement. She smiled and said, "You were there."[4]

We need to have a spirit which encourages others to feel free to share their burdens with us. And as we encourage others, our own depression can be lifted as well.

WHAT GOES AROUND, COMES AROUND.

Another help in dealing with depression is to recognize its cyclical nature. Most depression comes and goes. Often the cycle will pass, if we just give it time.

Have you ever noticed how depression often hits in the evening, when we are tired and most vulnerable? Many times, just going to bed and getting a good night's sleep will do wonders for depression. If you sense you are vulnerable to depression in the evenings, don't try to solve the world's problems when you are tired. Go to bed. Life will seem more manageable in the morning.

My wife, Ann, has had opportunities to do battle with the lion of depression. She went to bed one night discouraged and depressed. Around 2:00 A.M., the Holy Spirit brought to her mind the question, "Why are you cast down, and why are you disquieted within?" She knew this was Scripture, but was not sure from which of the psalms it came. Early the next morning, she found the words in Psalm 42:5-6:

> Why are you cast down, O my soul,
>   and why are you disquieted within me?
> Hope in God; for I shall again praise him,
>   my help and my God.

She realized that God was saying to her, "Your hope is in me—remember me, and *this too will pass.* You will again praise me."

Depression can come in cycles as a result of circumstances. If we can realize that we are going through the "valley of the shadow of death," and still keep on going and believing that we will come through it, our times of depression can be less stark and edged with hope. King David found hope in God in his times of discouragement and depression:

> Even though I walk through the valley of the shadow of death,
>   I fear no evil;
> for thou art with me;
>   thy rod and thy staff,
>   they comfort me. (Ps. 23:4)

Florence Chadwick was a famed swimmer who first failed and then succeeded in swimming across the Catalina Channel between California and an island off the coast. The first time she attempted the feat, the weather conditions were atrocious. She had to swim for hours in chilly water, with fog so thick she barely could see in any direction. Severe fatigue set in, and finally she said, "I can't go any farther." Fifteen hours and fifty-five minutes from the time she entered the water, they picked her up in a rescue boat. She found out later that she had stopped short of her goal, only thirty minutes from the mainland.

She made this statement: "I was not defeated by the chill of the water or by the fatigue of my own body; I was defeated by the fog that kept me from seeing my objective. I could have made another half-mile."

Two months later she swam the distance successfully and established the record for women, two hours faster than any man had swum that channel. This time she held on through the fog and refused to let it defeat her.

Remember that much depression will cycle away. Just when things seem most impossible, hope is around the corner. By holding on a little longer, we may be able to defeat the lion of depression.

YOU ARE NEVER ALONE.

The noted lyricist Oscar Hammerstein wrote the words to a well-known musical, *Carousel*, during World War II. During the difficult circumstances of the war—with its misery and death—he wrote the lyrics to "You'll Never Walk Alone":

> When you walk through a storm,
>   hold your head up high,
> And don't be afraid of the dark.
> At the end of the storm is a golden sky,
> And the sweet, silver song of a lark.
>
> Walk on through the wind,
> Walk on through the rain,

Though your dreams be tossed and blown.
Walk on, walk on, with hope in your heart,
And you'll never walk alone.

No storm or darkness shall daunt the human spirit.

Most of us have suffered, or will suffer, from feelings of depression, and we come into daily contact with persons who suffer from depression. We may even be in the midst of a depressed time right now! The depression may be related to a genetic chemical imbalance, a physical problem that brings on a chemical imbalance in our bodies, or circumstances beyond or even under our control. Whatever the cause, *God has not left us alone to deal with our depression.*

Fear not, for I am with you,
  be not dismayed, for I am your God;
I will strengthen you, I will help you,
  I will uphold you with my victorious right hand. (Isa. 41:10)

Fear not, for I have redeemed you;
  I have called you by name, you are mine.
When you pass through the waters I will be with you;
  and through the rivers, they shall not overwhelm you;
when you walk through fire you shall not be burned,
  and the flame shall not consume you.
For I am the LORD your God,
  the Holy One of Israel, your Savior. (Isa. 43:1b-3)

God has sent support persons to help us—in our family, in our church, and in the medical profession. We have been promised that God will never leave us or forsake us (Deut. 31:6; Heb. 13:5), and the Holy Spirit has been sent to help us in our weakness. God has provided us with words of encouragement in the Scriptures, to keep us going in the darkest of nights and to give us hope for better days ahead. God has loved us with a joy unspeakable, so that we can lower our perfectionist expectations for ourselves and others, and be about the business of reconciliation and forgiveness.

In your times of depression, remember the value God has placed on your life; rejoice in your gifts. Serve others and their needs. Don't wallow in self-pity. By being secure in the knowledge that you are a beloved child of God, you can turn your times of depression into positive experiences as you build your faith in God, your character, and your service to others. "Thanks be to God, who gives us the victory through our Lord Jesus Christ" (I Cor. 15:57).

JOURNAL JOTS

For Fun: The most recent time I felt depressed: _____

_____

_____

For Discovery: Jesus experienced times of lowness in heart and spirit. See his response to Herod's execution of John the Baptist in Matthew 14:1-13, and his feelings in the garden of Gethsemane (Matt. 26:37). Read chapter 53 of Isaiah. How might Jesus have experienced depression here on earth?

_____

_____

How does the suffering of Jesus help me in my times of suffering? (See Heb. 4:14-16) _____

_____

What good things have come from a time when I experienced depression? _____

_____

_____

For Commitment This Week: My plan of action to combat the current or next depression in my life: _____

_____

_____

The Lion of Resentment
I WON'T Forget That!

PERSONAL INVENTORY: Do you carry any grudges?

Place a check by any of the following circumstances—past or present—which may have caused you to form grudges against yourself, someone else, and/or God.

_____ 1. One of your family members died.

_____ 2. Someone close to you has suffered greatly.

_____ 3. You lost your job.

_____ 4. You never have enough money for the things you need.

_____ 5. You've undergone an endless series of troublesome circumstances.

_____ 6. You were betrayed by a good friend.

_____ 7. You were cheated.

_____ 8. Someone in your church hurt your feelings.

_____ 9. Your prayer was not answered in the way you expected.

_____10. A minister or religious leader let you down.

_____11. No one gave you the second chance you deserved.

_____12. You experienced loneliness.

_____13. Someone else got all the "breaks."

_____14. You found out about an opportunity too late.

_____15. Your health prevented you from doing what you wanted.

_____16. You feel you missed the chance of a lifetime because you were the wrong age, sex, or race.

_____17. You feel shortchanged on your appearance.

_____18. You feel shortchanged on your talents and abilities.

_____19. You feel shortchanged with your spouse.

_____20. Your children have made life difficult for you.

The biggest resentment you are dealing with now: _____

_____

_____

_____

WHY, GOD? WHY ME?

I remember the first church I pastored while I was still in seminary, soon to be married. When the parsonage committee decided to fix up the parsonage, several extended families volunteered to sponsor one room each to bring the home up to "minimum standards." One family's room did not have a bulb in its light fixture, so that family borrowed a bulb from another family's room—and forgot to return it. That began a great civil war! The feud between the two families quickly mushroomed as their friends took sides. It lasted for months. I soon found that these people did not easily let go of a grievance; in fact, they almost seemed to enjoy licking their old wounds.

Holding on to grudges and resentments takes a concentrated effort. We need to go to a great extent to nurse a grudge, to remember why we're so angry or upset, to persuade ourselves of its magnitude, and to rekindle the flame of passion should it begin to wane. Yet we continue to carry grudges long enough to damage ourselves, our relationships with others, and even with God. What makes us hang on to our resentments? Why do we often allow grievances to consume much of our conscious thought?

For some reason, nursing a grudge can feel good at first. Do you remember the story of the woman bitten by a mad dog? Her doctor told her she had only a few hours to live, and she had better begin preparations for her funeral. So she immediately began to make a list of friends and acquaintances. Curious, her doctor asked if these were people who would be recipients of her estate.

She replied, "No, these are people I want to bite!"

Nursing grudges becomes second nature when we cultivate feelings of self-pity! After all, life isn't fair! Many opportunities have passed us by. We're not as physically attractive or as financially secure as our neighbor. Our friends have neglected us. We've had more than our share of unhappy circumstances. So we begin to develop seeds of hurt which grow into full-size weeds of resentment. What we often fail to realize is that actually, we are hurting ourselves when we hold on to our grievances.

The famous Methodist missionary, author, and lecturer E. Stanley Jones once stated that he felt that 65 percent of all physical sickness is related to feelings of resentment, hate, and bitterness. A West Coast surgeon increased Jones's statistics: He feels that 85 percent of sickness is caused by deep resentments of which people cannot rid themselves.

I have known people who have developed hives, ulcers, and

87

all sorts of ailments because they have allowed bitterness and grievances to consume their lives. I've seen red-faced men, scowling women, and unhappy children—all nursing grudges against someone. I have seen it even in the life of the church.

Judas' life was changed irreparably when he allowed the resentment he carried against Jesus to fester. His Master had disappointed him. This "Son of God" was not the king he expected. *His* Messiah would have established a powerful earthly kingdom. Judas' misunderstandings and hurts gave way to bitter disillusionment, and he allowed himself to be sold out to wrongdoing. But then by his final act of suicide, he refused to give himself a second chance.

Not only can nursing grudges wreak havoc with our physical bodies, but it can affect our relationships with others, causing heartache, loneliness, or loss of self-esteem. We can waste precious years of what might have been a treasured friendship. By refusing to forgive others, we can inhibit the frequency of God's reconciliatory grace flowing through us.

I have seen it happen again and again. Throughout my ministry, I have witnessed scores of persons who have been hurt by others and carry grievances. A couple of years ago a lovely young woman came to my office to tell me her story. She had been married the year before, and her closest friend had failed to come to her wedding. Angered and hurt, the newlywed refused to speak to or see her friend. About eleven months after the wedding, she ran into her friend at the grocery store. They came unavoidably face to face. As they were forced to communicate, they found themselves catching up on old times. The friend explained why she had missed the wedding and they forgave each other. They recognized with sadness the joys of friendship they had missed because each had continued to nurse a grievance toward the other.

Remember the story of Jacob and Esau? Admittedly, Esau had been tricked by his brother. But he allowed resentment to settle in his heart:

Now Esau hated Jacob because of the blessing with which his father had blessed him, and Esau said to himself, "The days of mourning for my father are approaching; then I will kill my brother Jacob." (Gen. 27:41)

Rebekah, their mother, got wind of Esau's plans and advised Jacob to get out of town—quickly! For many years, the two brothers missed the camaraderie of a sibling relationship. When they finally were reconciled many years later, they wept and rejoiced. What a number of wasted years they had allowed to pass as they allowed resentment to grow.

NIP IT IN THE BUD!

So we admit that holding a grudge hurts ourselves and others. What do we do about it? How can we prevent grudges from developing in the first place?

First of all, *minimize your disappointment in others by recognizing that no one is perfect.* It is inevitable that persons will hurt you. Some will intentionally cause you trouble; others will mean no harm, but their actions or lack of actions will cause you problems. When you are involved with others, you set yourself up for hurt and disappointment as well as for happiness. The only way to minimize your disappointment in others is to love them in spite of their weaknesses and actions.

Jesus knew human nature. That's why he spoke of certain weapons we can use to fight against feelings of resentment:

You have heard that it was said, "You shall love your neighbor and hate your enemy." But I say to you, Love your enemies and pray for those who persecute you, so that you may be sons of your Father who is in heaven; for he makes his sun rise on the evil and on the good, and sends rain on the just and on the unjust. For if you love those who love you, what reward have you? Do not even the tax collectors do the same? And if you salute only your brethren, what more are you doing than others? Do not even the Gentiles do the same? (Matt. 5:43-47)

Why do you see the speck that is in your brother's eye, but do not notice the log that is in your own eye? Or how can you say to your brother, "Let me take the speck out of your eye," when there is the log in your own eye? You hypocrite, first take the log out of your own eye, and then you will see clearly to take the speck out of your brother's eye. (Matt. 7:3-5)

We can love people as they are when we look to God for our "strokes." We don't need to depend upon others to give us our self-esteem. We don't thrive because of the approval of others. We can free ourselves from the bondage of human expectation and look to God for unmerited love and approval.

Karen Burton Mains, in *With My Whole Heart: Disciplines for Strengthening the Inner Life*, discusses "the discipline of choosing freedom from the need for human approval":

So I began to attempt to do my work for Christ alone. I refused honorariums for a year and followed harder after Him. I ventured into harder and more arduous prayer exercises and purposely neglected to mention my journeys to friends. I practiced doing secret acts of Christian love, small gifts and kindnesses for others, without signing my name or without pointing to my own benevolences. I prepared dinners for guests as though I was cooking food for one Guest alone. I learned to look to Him for His approval and to be content with His words, "Well done."[1]

As we love our friends and our enemies alike, we develop fewer resentments and cultivate more understanding. We begin to concentrate on our common bond of membership in the family of God. We concentrate on our positive relationships with others, rather than on the many ways they may have failed us. We look to God, rather than to people, to meet our needs and expectations. And we notice that the heavy burden of grievances we carry becomes lighter with each passing day.

SET IN CLAY, OR IN STONE?

All of us could take a lesson from two little girls who were featured a number of years ago on "Candid Camera." The host had set up the girls in a disagreement over whose daddy was the best. They began to argue, but the camera malfunctioned and the dialogue was temporarily stopped. After the camera was fixed, the host tried to recreate the disagreement, but the little girls could not remember it.

He continued to bait them with, "Wasn't *your* daddy stronger (or wiser) than hers?" Neither of the girls could be drawn into the argument because they had become friends during the time the camera was being repaired. Their life was changed for the better because neither was capable of carrying a grudge for more than a few moments.

We could handle our grievances better if we did not allow them an opportunity to set. *One of the best ways to keep a hurt from becoming a full-blown resentment is to quickly forgive the person who has hurt you.* We need to be immediate with *our* forgiveness, even if *we* are the offended party. We need to apologize and make restitution, even if *we* are the offended party. We can offer others a second chance.

You may say, "Hey, that isn't fair!" or "How can you expect me to do *that?*" Forgiveness is a strange thing. Often it begins as a mental process. There may be no way to *feel* we want to forgive someone who has offended us. However, as we begin the mental process of forgiveness—as we realize that God through Jesus Christ forgave us our sins, and therefore we are required to forgive others their sins—we put into motion the spirit of reconciliation. As we mentally offer forgiveness to others, feelings of love and grace will come.

Think of the biblical characters—certainly undeserving—who demonstrate the power of a second chance.

The apostle Peter hardly deserved a second chance. After he had walked and talked with Jesus for three years, seemingly his closest friend, who understood Jesus' mission more clearly than did others, Peter turned around and let him down! How could he deny his Lord, and three times at that? Yet Jesus' response is most remarkable. He asks Peter to recommit himself and reaffirm his love. Then Jesus says, "Follow me." Jesus allows Peter to repent and begin life anew, with no strings attached (see John 21).

Consider Paul. God gave him a second chance! He had been a zealot and murderer, yet God offered him a new life. The leaders in the early church were not eager to give Saul a second chance. They were too afraid! But Barnabas embraced Saul and was willing to give him the benefit of the doubt. In a sense, the church is what it is today because of Barnabas' willingness to risk his life for Saul. That kind of action allows the world to be turned upside down!

What about John Mark? That young nephew of Paul wanted the excitement of going on a missionary journey! But shortly after he left with Paul and Barnabas, John Mark decided, for one reason or another, that he didn't want to continue. So in Perga, John left their company and returned to Jerusalem (Acts 13:13). Later, when Paul wanted to return to the churches they previously had visited to check up on the believers, Barnabas suggested that they include John Mark, but Paul disagreed—he didn't want to be involved with him again! So they decided to separate into two groups: Barnabas took John Mark and sailed to Cyprus; Paul and Silas headed for Syria and Cilicia (Acts 15:36-41). However, in Paul's later ministry, he mentions John Mark as being a very useful servant (II Tim. 4:11). Thank God for Barnabas, who was willing to give John Mark a second chance! We need more "Barnabas-living" today!

THE BITTER-ROOT SYNDROME

John and Paula Sandford, in *Transformation of the Inner Man*, discuss an interesting aspect of grudge-bearing which they refer to as the bitter-root syndrome. They detail the problem of harboring resentment against a family member. They explain that often, persons who grow up resenting a family member for a particular reason can eventually become like that very family member. For example, a child may dislike the fact that the father is always late and cannot be counted on, or that the mother never gives enough of her time. If the child continues to allow this resentment to build, continues to judge the parent, a seed of dishonor is sown. This seed, if allowed to build and fester, will return to be reaped when the child becomes an adult. As this programmed pattern develops in the years ahead, the same characteristic will appear in the grown child or in a mate. In other words, the longer a judgment continues, the greater it becomes.

> See to it that no one fail to obtain the grace of God; that no "root of bitterness" spring up and cause trouble, and by it the many become defiled. (Heb. 12:15)

> Judge not, that you be not judged. For with the judgment you pronounce you will be judged, and the measure you give will be the measure you get. (Matt. 7:1-2)

> Do not be deceived; God is not mocked, for whatever a man sows, that he will also reap. (Gal. 6:7)

The only hope to break this "bitter-root" cycle is to consciously forgive the offending family member, to exchange the "dividing wall of hostility for the cross of Christ." We may not be able to love the person who has hurt us, but God can love that person through us, and God can show us how to express our forgiveness. Jesus has paid the full legal demand and can set us free from resentments and bitter roots, if we will just give him the chance. In fact, "bitter roots are normally not taken care of until we invite Jesus to accomplish that specific task."[2]

> The blessed end of transformation of bitter roots is first that we find ourselves continually surprised. Things just don't happen

like they used to. . . . Things begin to work together for good, visibly. . . .

Perhaps the most blessed shock is that often the very people we have been hating become the ones we love or appreciate the most. We even become grateful for their former persecuting ways (or whatever they did) because by that we saw and were set free. Life takes on a new lease. It is as though new vistas open before us—and we come (slowly perhaps) to realize they were there all along; we just couldn't see them. What used to bother us now falls like water off a duck's back. We giggle instead of tense up. We laugh *with* those we used to get mad at for laughing *at* us. And we see others and our own self with real compassion.

Truly in that area we are born anew.[3]

CAN GOD LET YOU DOWN?

A final way to keep resentments from building is to *minimize our disappointment with God.* That may sound like a strange piece of advice, but it's very important! Many times we set ourselves up to be disappointed in God because we are too presumptuous—we tell God how to answer our prayers and how to run our lives. Then when our prayers are not answered the way *we* thought was best, we feel God has let us down. Our faith begins to falter, we wonder if God really cares, and the seeds for resentment are sown.

When my wife mentions a "spiritual fatality," she is referring to a person who loses faith because God does not respond the way the person expected. She always becomes concerned when someone in the church becomes ill, and others pray for the person and then announce that this person will be healed. Yes, sometimes that happens. But at other times, for reasons we cannot explain, the person is not healed until he or she crosses from this life to the next. Then, invariably, because of others' careless conversation, a "spiritual fatality" will result. Someone will make the faulty assumption that because the sick member was not healed, God must be inept, absent, or uncaring.

Have you reached the level of spiritual maturity to understand that God will not always answer prayers the way you wish? Can you say,

> God, I don't understand, but I trust you to do the best thing for my life and the lives of others. I know I can share with you the desires of my heart, but I dare not tell you exactly how to run my life. I trust your wisdom and mercy in all areas.

If you can say that, you will find that your faith will be strong, even in times of trouble.

> But who are you, a man, to answer back to God? Will what is molded say to its molder, "Why have you made me thus?" Has the potter no right over the clay, to make out of the same lump one vessel for beauty and another for menial use? (Rom. 9:20-21)

> Thy kingdom come,
> Thy will be done,
>   on earth as it is in heaven. (Matt. 6:10)

O may we seek God's will, and not that of our own presumptuous desires!

FORGIVENESS, IN ITS RAREST FORM

A true incident involved a parish priest in the Philippine Islands. While the priest was in seminary, he had committed a terrible sin. He had asked for forgiveness, but ever since, he wondered if God had ever really forgiven him. One day a very religious woman told the priest that she often had visions from God, that she talked to Christ and Christ would talk to her.

The priest decided to give her a test: "Ask Jesus what sin I committed in seminary."

A number of days later when the woman returned, the priest eagerly asked, "Did you have a vision from Jesus?"

"Oh, yes," she said. "He talked with me and I talked with him."

"What, then, was my terrible sin?"

"Jesus said, 'I don't remember.' "

God, through Jesus Christ, bore all ill feelings, all bitternesses, and all resentments at Calvary. "I am He who blots out your transgressions for my own sake, and I will not remember your sins" (Isa. 43:25). On that tree when he suffered and died for you and me, he released all grievances, once and for all. Surely, we can use him as our example. In his purity, he forgave those who wished him harm. His sacrifice allows us to have a regenerated life. How much more should we be willing to pass that hope on to others! In the words of the psalmist:

The LORD is merciful and gracious,
    slow to anger and abounding in steadfast love.
He will not always chide,
    nor will he keep his anger for ever.
He does not deal with us according to our sins,
    nor requite us according to our iniquities.
For as the heavens are high above the earth,
    so great is his steadfast love toward those who fear him;
as far as the east is from the west,
    so far does he remove our transgressions from us.
As a father pities his children,
    so the LORD pities those who fear him. (Ps. 103:8-13)

JOURNAL JOTS

For Fun: My most embarrassing moment in elementary school:

_____

_____

My most recent embarrassing moment: _____

_____

_____

For Discovery: Read Leviticus 19:17-18. What command do these verses give? _____

_____

_____

How does the coming of Jesus give you power and hope to carry out the above command? (See Hebrews 4:14-16.)

_____

_____

For Commitment This Week: Make a list of any persons you need to forgive. Resolve to begin praying for those persons every day this week.

My plan of reconciliation: _____

_____

_____

CHAPTER VII

The Lion of Anger
Self-controlled? Or Out of Control?

PERSONAL INVENTORY: Analyze your anger.

Circle the letter of the answer that best describes your response to the following statements:

1. When I am angry, I resemble:

    a) an exploding volcano.
    b) a pouting child.
    c) a bottled-up volcano.
    d) a crybaby.

2. I usually become angry when:
    a) things don't go my way.
    b) someone disagrees with me.
    c) someone hurts my feelings.
    d) I am reminded that life isn't fair.

3. The last time someone was angry with me, I:

    a) hunched my back and hissed back.
    b) nursed my wounds for days.
    c) retreated like a dog with its tail between its legs.
    d) smiled and kept going.

4. I become angry:

    a) several times each day.   c) a few times a week.

    b) about once a month.   d) once in a blue moon.

5. After I am angry, I feel:

    a) ashamed.   c) sad.

    b) embarrassed.   d) as if a load has been lifted off my chest.

6. When someone is angry with me, I:

    a) act as if I don't care.   c) try to defend myself.

    b) get even angrier at them.   d) feel sorry for myself.

7. I usually stay angry:

    a) for a few minutes.   c) for a few hours.

    b) for a few days.   d) for weeks at a time.

8. I think I have a right to be angry when:

    a) someone has taken advantage of me.   c) my children have been insulted.

    b) my character has been misrepresented.   d) my values have been challenged.

9. I usually get angry at the people:

    a) I love most.   c) I don't know.

    b) I know only as acquaintances.

10. I think righteous anger is O.K. if:

    a) I don't get *too* angry.   c) I apologize later.

    b) I am defending my honor.   d) I am defending the Lord's honor.

ANGER OF THE WORST SORT

Alexander the Great conquered most of the known world in his day. At a banquet in Persia one evening following a day of heavy fighting, one of his generals, Cletus, became irritated by a remark made by Alexander. Cletus retaliated with a taunt, and in a fit of anger, Alexander grabbed a spear and hurled it at Cletus. The spear left a fatal wound. At once Alexander realized what he had done. Cletus—childhood friend, companion, one-time rescuer of his life—lay dead. Alexander drew out the fatal spear and, but for his officers, would have thrust it into himself. All that night and for days afterward, he lay writhing on his bed, calling out the name of his friend. Alexander overcame almost every known city of the ancient world, yet was not able to subdue the more important "city"—his own angry spirit.

Alexander's story is tragic, but certainly not unique. Many lives have been destroyed by the lion of unbridled anger. Anger often is exhibited when and where we least expect it, even by those of us striving to fit into the semi-saint category. There is much truth to the old saying, "To live with a saint in heaven will be a thing of glory, but to live with a saint on earth is quite another story."

As we recall angry episodes, we are amazed by our foolishness and possibly even wonder whether God is commenting, "Is that *really* my child?"

Some incidents still claim a place in my memory. In the post office near one of my student churches, the Sunday school superintendent and the mayor had a fist fight over a church matter. A leading layman became so angry at a time of revival that while the music of "When the Saints Go Marching In" sounded through the doors, he left the imprint of his fist in the wall. Did these Christians lose sight of the fact that the anger of men and women does not work the righteousness of God? (James 1:20). Or is this what happens when our flesh is allowed to run rampant?

There was the memorable Annual Conference in Dallas when we had recessed for the evening meal. As everyone rushed to eat, I set out on a freeway service road, where I met a car going the wrong way. I made loud use of my horn and flailed an arm to communicate my indignation at the other driver's stupidity. Out of all the thousands of people in Dallas, would you believe that I had poured out my impatient spirit upon my very own bishop?

Sometimes we provoke others to anger. There was the Sunday my diligent and efficient wife was preparing the noon meal for our family and extended family. While the men watched the latest Cowboy football fumble on TV and the women looked at pictures, my wife was struggling alone in the kitchen. After many calls to dinner, we finally responded, and as Ann removed the roast from the oven, she somehow managed to dump the entire thing on the carpet. We were so dumbfounded we didn't move fast enough, and Ann unleashed her lioness spirit on all of us—"Quit sitting there like crows and help me! If you had been helping me, this wouldn't have happened!"—among other incriminating and deserved sentences. We had provoked her to anger.

I suspect that you also could compile a list of times when anger got the best of you. Anger is a natural bodily response to hurt, frustration, or fear, and dealing with it is a part of life. According to Scripture, anger becomes negative when one of two things happens:

1. When it is allowed to remain, or
2. When it is expressed in hurtful and out-of-control ways.

WHEN ANGER IS ALLOWED TO REMAIN

I mentioned the first kind of negative anger in chapter 6. *When we permit the sun to set on our anger, we are asking for problems.* Anger that is allowed to fester becomes hate. In *Forgive and Forget,* Lewis B. Smedes points out the important difference between anger and hate:

> We must not confuse hate with anger. It is hate and not anger that needs healing.
>
> Anger is a sign that we are alive and well. Hate is a sign that we are sick and need to be healed.
>
> Healthy anger drives us to do something to change what makes us angry; anger can energize us to make things better. Hate does not want to change things for the better; it wants to make things worse. Hate wants to belch the foul breath of death over a life that love alone creates.[1]

The way to rid ourselves of hate is to forgive. Even though I have talked about it in previous chapters, I want to offer some new thoughts on forgiveness as it relates to anger. Even when our mind says we have "forgiven" a person who wronged us, we often feel we have failed, because our emotions still remember the anger and hurt we felt at the time. What we need to realize is that although we *forgive,* we usually do not *forget.* Just because I have forgiven someone for a thoughtless remark, it doesn't necessarily mean that my conscious mind forgets the remark. And yet, because my mind *can* remember the offensive remark, it doesn't mean that I haven't forgiven the person.

Memory is a part of our brain function, a God-given ability. Our intricate web of memories is not like a slate that we can just wipe clean. So although we may remember an incident, we have begun the process of consciously forgiving the person associated with that experience. Forgiveness offers us a way to minimize the pain associated with a thoughtless act (or whatever we find it necessary to forgive), and to get on with our life and ministry. We can see persons who have wronged us in a new light of compassion, not necessarily justifying their acts toward us, but releasing both them and ourselves from the negative situation, toward healing and reconciliation.

Several passages of Scripture begin to make more sense when

we understand forgiveness in this way. "Do not let the sun go down on your anger" (Eph. 4:26) makes clear that we won't be able to resolve all conflict and forget each incident when we go to bed. However, we can carry forth the mental process of forgiveness each day. We can pray, "God, I forgive, just as you freely forgave me in Christ. Now help me to work with this person to resolve our differences and move forward together."

When Peter asked Jesus, "Lord, how often shall my brother sin against me, and I forgive him?" and Jesus answered, "Seventy times seven" (Matt. 18:21-22), it becomes obvious that after repeatedly forgiving someone, we won't totally *forget* what happened. The events may be clear in our conscious memory each time we encounter this person. However, God begins to remove the pain of the situation, and we allow God to continue to work in our lives because of our free spirit of forgiveness. In time, if we do not dwell on our hurt, the angering event will become less and less etched in our memories.

One fact is important: Just because we forgive a person, or a person forgives us, does not mean that all consequences which result from the incident are revoked. God has set our world to operate very carefully within certain laws. Actions produce reactions, and forgiveness does not remove all consequences.

For example, let's say that a parent becomes angry with a teacher in a church-related private school, and that parent withdraws the child from the school. Later, the parent wants to reconcile with the teacher. They meet together, each explains his or her side of the story, and they extend forgiveness to each other. The parent then decides to reenroll the child in the school. But in the meantime, the class has filled up. There is now no room for the child.

Does this mean that the teacher has not forgiven the parent, or that the parent has not forgiven the teacher? No! Forgiveness has occurred, but the consequences of the action are still in operation.

Consider divorce. When a divorce occurs, much pain and

suffering result. Even if one or both parties have forgiven the other, that forgiveness does not erase the reality of the divorce. The children still must divide their lives between the two parents, the pain of separation is still felt, healing must occur, and on and on.

We must remember that forgiveness is not a "good feeling," not is it a miraculous "memory eraser." The act of forgiveness is a conscious prayer on our part toward God, to change our angry spirit toward the offender. Only then will the pain and anger associated with an offending act gradually begin to diminish.

THE SNOWBALLING EFFECT

I want to focus the rest of this chapter on the second abuse of anger: *When anger is expressed in out-of-control ways.* The Scriptures give us several examples of persons who allowed their anger to sway out of control.

When Cain and Abel brought their offerings, the Lord had "no regard" for Cain's offering of the fruit of the ground.

> So Cain was very angry, and his countenance fell. The LORD said to Cain, "Why are you angry, and why has your countenance fallen? If you do well, will you not be accepted? And if you do not do well, sin is lurking at the door; its desire is for you, but you must master it." (Gen. 4:5b-7)

But Cain failed to master his anger. He took Abel out to the field and killed him.

Moses gives us a good example of anger which God felt was out of control. Moses missed entering the Promised Land because of his anger and disobedience. He struck a rock twice in anger, as he looked for water for the rebellious Israelites (Num. 20:10-12).

Perhaps anger led Saul into his melancholy. He heard the crowds shouting that although he had killed thousands, David had killed tens of thousands. And out of jealousy and anger, he threw a spear to try to end the life of David. Saul's uncontrollable anger forced David to flee for his life (I Sam. 18–24).

Most of us have had times in our lives when we allowed our anger to get out of control. As a result, we have embarrassed ourselves, wounded others, and harmed our witness for the Lord.

Anger may be a natural response, but how we respond to that anger becomes an exercise of our will. How can we get a better handle on our anger? How can we channel it toward good? How can we cultivate a measure of control over our angry feelings?

"BE ANGRY, BUT SIN NOT."

Be angry, but sin not;
   commune with your own hearts on your beds, and be silent.
                                        (Ps. 4:4)

A soft answer turns away wrath,
but a harsh word stirs up anger. (Prov. 15:1)

Let every man be quick to hear, slow to speak, slow to anger, for the anger of man does not work the righteousness of God.
                                    (James 1:19-20)

Let all bitterness and wrath and anger and clamor and slander be put away from you, with all malice, and be kind to one another, tenderhearted, forgiving one another, as God in Christ forgave you. (Eph. 4:31-32)

One of the hardest things for us to do in the face of anger is to be still. Dr. James Dobson, in *Emotions: Can You Trust Them?* describes his own struggle in this area.

He mentions that when he was a young man he handled his anger and aggression by perfecting "the art of verbal combat to a high level of proficiency." However, as he matured in the Lord, he knew the Lord was calling his behavior into harmony with God's Word. And one day, "divine providence" put his responses to the test.

Because Easter Sunday was imminent, he had decided to surprise his wife with an Easter corsage, and accordingly placed his order with the local florist the first of the week. When he went to pick up his corsage on Saturday afternoon, the saleslady informed him that they would not be able to fill his order after all. As he questioned her, a large red-faced man burst through the door from the shop at the rear of the building. The burly man proceeded to unload his anger—both physical and verbal—upon Dr. Dobson. It took every bit of self-control he could summon, but somehow he managed to utter a meager defensive reply and walk out of the shop. Later, as he looked back on his restraint with some satisfaction, he realized it had been his wisest option![2]

Let's bring the situation a little closer to home. Here you are, trembling with rage; you are angry; something wrong has occurred; you are at the edge and about to respond; how can you keep your anger under control? The above Scripture passage gives you part of the answer: *Wait. Allow time to pass. Meditate in your heart and be still. Do not respond in the spirit of anger. Stop. Slow down. Think it through.*

During the Civil War, President Lincoln became very upset with one of his officers, General Meade. Meade had allowed General Lee to make a safe retreat from Gettysburg across the Potomac River into Virginia. For one reason or another, Meade had not been able to keep up with Lee. Lincoln became quite angry, so he sat down and wrote Meade a hot letter. But the letter was never sent. He had vented his anger by writing the letter, so after contemplating and reflecting, he decided not to send it.

It is difficult for most of us to wait and think, instead of moving forward and acting. Much in our society today encourages us to take up for ourselves, not let ourselves be pushed around, and if we don't look out for ourselves, who will? There are times when we do need to move forward and act accordingly. But in the heat of anger, we need to respond cautiously, so as not to fan the fuel of fury, which will cause us much more heartache later.

Maybe you have found that counting to ten is a valuable tool in managing your anger. Remove yourself from the situation, if possible, and ask for God's help—this will do wonders for your self-control. Even if you cannot remove yourself from the situation, postpone any verbal responses until you have had time to think them through and pray. Try to view the circumstances through the eyes of the other party. Just allowing time to pass before you react will tame the lion of your angry spirit.

PUNISHMENT—THE ULTIMATE WEAPON

When we are angry, one of the hardest things to do is to be still. And it is *even harder to repay good for evil.* What a seemingly unnatural response! Yet, that is precisely what Paul tells the church at Rome to do:

> Bless those who persecute you; bless and do not curse them. Rejoice with those who rejoice, weep with those who weep. Live in harmony with one another; do not be haughty, but associate with the lowly; never be conceited. Repay no one evil for evil, but take thought for what is noble in the sight of all. If possible, so far as it depends upon you, live peaceably with all. Beloved, never avenge yourselves, but leave it to the wrath of God; for it is written, "Vengeance is mine, I will repay, says the Lord." No, "if your enemy is hungry, feed him; if he is thirsty, give him drink; for by so doing you will heap burning coals upon his head." Do not be overcome by evil, but overcome evil with good. (Rom. 12:14-21)

Why is it so hard for us to realize that we do not need to seek vengeance toward those who have angered us? If we are willing to be honest, we probably fail to trust God enough. We think it is up to us to make sure that the balances are weighed—that we get our fair share and others receive their fair judgment. What a ludicrous, myopic view!

On the contrary, we know that justice is one of God's inherent characteristics. God does not need our help in balancing the scales of life.

> For we know him who said, "Vengeance is mine, I will repay." And again, "The Lord will judge his people." It is a fearful thing to fall into the hands of the living God. (Heb. 10:30-31)

> I will betroth you to me in righteousness and in justice, in steadfast love, and in mercy. (Hos. 2:19-b)

We begin to trust God when we leave matters of vengeance to our Creator. The affairs of God's world will be managed in a way and time of God's choosing. God will handle matters of punishment, whether it be on this earth, in terms of cause and effect, or whether it be in terms of eternal judgment.

This does not mean that we do not seek for justice on earth. And it doesn't mean that we fail to work for right causes. But it does mean that we do not allow our anger to force us to get back at every person who does us wrong. We don't always need to have the last word. Not seeking retaliation frees us to be about the business of sharing the gospel of Jesus Christ with others. Not being vengeful actually allows us the opportunity to return good for evil, love for hate, a blessing for a curse.

Be a lion tamer! Practice being a peacemaker. Isn't that the response our Lord expects of us?

RETURNING GOOD FOR EVIL

Pastors in ministry for many years, as I have been, have many opportunities to repay evil with good, if we so choose. I have known a few people who accused me unjustly (or so I thought!). In fact, I have been accused of almost everything: "Not preaching enough from the Bible," "preaching too much Scripture," "not being born again," "being too spiritual," "not caring about the welfare of the local church," "being too Methodist," and "not being Methodist enough." The list could go on and on. When I am "unjustly" accused, my natural response is to defend myself immediately, to verbally persuade the accusers of their erring judgment. Sometimes that approach works, and communication is often important. However, many times a defense presented to an offending party is like water poured on a duck's back, or even fuel added to a fire. What then? How do I respond in Christian love?

Often the next step is to move from words to actions. I simply must show those people how wrong I feel their accusations are. I continue to live my life—preach from the Bible, walk daily with the Lord, care about the church, work for reform within The United Methodist Church—and give any critics time to evaluate my character and life's statement. In the meantime, I go out of my way to show that I care. If there is a crisis in the family of an accuser, I respond with love. I offer more love than they can shake a stick at. (Isn't that what it means to "heap burning coals upon their heads"?) Usually they begin to change their opinions about me.

Easy? No! Do I always succeed? No! But each time I return good for evil, it gets a little easier. I begin to practice the gospel *toward* others. And I "press on toward the goal for the prize of the upward call of God in Christ Jesus" (Phil. 3:14).

CULTIVATING THE FRUITS OF MEEKNESS AND SELF-CONTROL

All of us are concerned about ourselves. Every subtle and outright message of secular society screams, "Look out for yourself—no one else will!" But the gospel calls us to a much different and more radical kind of self-love—a self-love so intertwined in God's love that we cannot help loving others. The gospel of Jesus always challenges us to be concerned for the needs of others, to the extent that we put others' needs ahead of our own.

I think that is the secret of controlling anger. When we cultivate an unselfish spirit of meekness, a spirit that says "I don't always need to have the last word" and "I can return good for evil," we develop a measure of self-control—to put it more accurately, the self becomes God-controlled. And God-control is the key to taming the lion of the angry spirit. When we lay our spirit down and take on the spirit of Christ, our trembling will cease and our faith in God will take over. The wild lion of anger will be bridled and tamed, and we can move on to accomplish God's will and way.

JOURNAL JOTS

For Fun: The event in my life that I remember made me most angry: _____

_____

I remember my response: _____

_____

For Discovery: Proverbs offers us several gems of wisdom in dealing with anger (see 14:16-17, 29; 16:32; 25:21-22). How does this advice help us when we face angering circumstances?

_____

Read Ephesians 4:31-32. What other responses can you make when you face angering situations? _____

_____

For Commitment This Week: The last time I felt my anger getting out of control: _____

_____

My plan of action for the next time I feel anger getting out of control:

1._____

2._____

3._____

VIII

The Lion of Worry

What If . . . Suppose . . .
I Should Have . . . Maybe . . .

PERSONAL INVENTORY: What are your biggest worries?

Rank your top five worries from the list below. You may add some of your own to the list if you wish.

_____	losing your job		threat of nuclear
	going into personal	_____	war
_____	debt		spread of
	the future of your	_____	secularism
_____	children		fulfillment of
	caring for aging	_____	career goals
_____	parents	_____	increasing crime
_____	getting older		drug and alcohol
	personal health	_____	abuse
_____	problems	_____	world hunger
_____	reality of death	_____	remaining single
_____	possible divorce	_____	other

Reflect upon your top five worries.

1. How many are strictly personal? _____

2. How many relate to others? _____

_____

3. Which do you discuss with friends? _____

_____

4. Which do you attempt to change? _____

_____

5. Which do you put at the top of your prayer list? _____

_____

TURBULENT, TROUBLED, OR TRANQUIL?

I was pretty upset. In fact, I was starting to be plain worried! My wife and I were scheduled to leave on vacation the next morning, and I was sick! Our travel itinerary included stops in three foreign countries. We were planning to be gone for nearly four weeks. About the last problem I needed the day before departure was a trip to the doctor! But who wants to be away from home, especially for an extended time in foreign countries, when one is ill?

My list of anxious thoughts could have filled a large diary! *What if* I am really sick on the plane? *Suppose* I become so ill I can't enjoy myself while away and wish I hadn't gone? I *should have* slowed down a few days earlier, and I might not have gotten sick in the first place. *Maybe* I should try to fit a doctor's appointment into my already overflowing last-minute list of things to do. *There's no way* I can possibly get ready to go, feeling as bad as I do!

Get the picture? The lion of worry had a hold on me! I'm not talking about a normal feeling of concern, which all of us feel from time to time. I'm talking about the crippling, debilitating form of worry that swallows you up in its sticky core—the kind of worry that carries no good purpose except to upset and unsettle.

At one time or another, all of us face this threatening lion of excessive worry. The old English root of the word *worry* means "to strangle." Chronic and excessive worry does just that. It makes us second-guess ourselves. It causes us to concern ourselves with things we cannot change and punish ourselves for decisions already made. It makes us anxious, troubled, annoyed, uneasy, choked, confused.

How can we more effectively manage the lion of worry? We can't reasonably remove ourselves from all circumstances that could cause us to worry. When we love and care for others, we will become involved with their concerns and problems. So we need to discover a way to put our worries into their proper perspective. We need to learn to trust God more, day by day, week by week, month by month, year by year. Bit by bit, we can begin to turn worry from a debilitating nightmare into a terrific training ground for our faith.

DO I HAVE THE POINT YET?

One of our biggest foes in trying to put our worries into an accurate perspective is that *we major in the minors of life.* Many of us are like the society woman who completed a course in first aid. She now felt prepared for any emergency that might come her way, and soon she had an opportunity to put what she had learned into practice.

She was standing on a street corner when three cars collided. Several persons were injured, and an onlooker called an ambulance.

The next day at a meeting of her bridge club, the woman told her friends about what had happened.

"For a moment, standing there on the curb, I didn't know what to do. Suddenly I remembered my Red Cross course, and I followed all the instructions just in time."

Her bridge partners were eager to hear all about the heroic measures she had attempted toward the injured.

She eagerly announced, "I sat right down on the curb, put my head down between my knees, and didn't even begin to faint!"

Just like that woman, we often get life out of perspective. We "major in the minors." In so doing, we miss the truly important matters in life.

WHAT IS REALLY IMPORTANT IN LIFE?

Sometimes we "major in the minors" because it is difficult to sort out what is really important. We might think that surely, food, clothing, and shelter are important. However, Jesus says that even these things are not worth our worried thoughts:

Therefore I tell you, do not be anxious about your life, what you shall eat or what you shall drink, nor about your body, what you shall put on. Is not life more than food, and the body more than clothing? Look at the birds of the air: they neither sow nor reap nor gather into barns, and yet your heavenly Father feeds them. Are you not of more value than they? And which of you by being anxious can add one cubit to his span of life?

And why are you anxious about clothing? Consider the lilies of the field, how they grow; they neither toil nor spin; yet I tell you, even Solomon in all his glory was not arrayed like one of these. But if God so clothes the grass of the field, which today is alive and tomorrow is thrown into the oven, will he not much more clothe you, O men of little faith?

Therefore do not be anxious, saying, "What shall we eat?" or "What shall we drink?" or "What shall we wear?" For the

Gentiles seek all these things; and your heavenly Father knows that you need them all. But seek first his kingdom and his righteousness, and all these things shall be yours as well. (Matt. 6:25-33)

If food, clothing, and shelter are things we need not worry about, what *is* important? Reread the last verse from the above passage: "Seek first his kingdom and his righteousness." When we take care of first things first, Jesus tells us that the other things in our lives will begin to line up.

How dare Jesus take such a lackadaisical view of food, clothing, and shelter? How can he tell us not to worry about our very sustenances of life? Probably because he understood the difference between major priorities and concerns of lesser significance. Jesus always challenged those he encountered to seek the kind of water that would cause them never to thirst again. He defined that "food" as doing God's will and work on this earth.

> Every one who drinks of this water will thirst again, but whoever drinks of the water that I shall give him will never thirst; the water that I shall give him will become in him a spring of water welling up to eternal life. (John 4:13-14)

> Meanwhile the disciples besought him, saying, "Rabbi, eat." But he said to them, "I have food to eat of which you do not know. . . . My food is to do the will of him who sent me, and to accomplish his work." (John 4:31-34)

Jesus is saying, "Why waste your life on earth by avidly worrying about everything that comes your way? Most things are not that important, when viewed in proportion to eternal matters. Use the energy you would use worrying about temporal matters to attend to matters of the soul."

> And [Jesus] said to them, "Take heed, and beware of all covetousness; for a man's life does not consist in the abundance

116

of his possessions." And he told them a parable, saying, "The land of a rich man brought forth plentifully; and he thought to himself, 'What shall I do, for I have nowhere to store my crops?' And he said, 'I will do this: I will pull down my barns, and build larger ones; and there I will store all my grain and my goods. And I will say to my soul, Soul, you have ample goods laid up for many years; take your ease, eat, drink, be merry.' But God said to him, 'Fool! This night your soul is required of you; and the things you have prepared, whose will they be?' So is he who lays up treasure for himself, and is not rich toward God."

And he said to his disciples, "Therefore I tell you, do not be anxious about your life, what you shall eat, nor about your body, what you shall put on. For life is more than food, and the body more than clothing." (Luke 12:15-23)

For what does it profit a man, to gain the whole world and forfeit his life? (Mark 8:36)

Oh, that we could view life as Jesus did! He had his "majors" and "minors" straight. It's not that Jesus didn't know that we need food to keep our bodies alive and healthy; he knew that overemphasis on food would cause us to become slothful and overweight. It's not that Jesus didn't think we needed a place to lay our head; he knew that building bigger and better houses could become a god to us. It's not that Jesus refused to recognize our need to be clothed; he knew the danger of materialism at the expense of the needy. His words were given to help us put the concerns of our lives into their true perspective. His words were given to guide us to emphasize the major chords in life, thereby freeing us to live more victoriously.

Every day I have a chance to put this into practice. Am I worried about how I look on a particular day, or to whom I will minister? Have I picked a fight with my wife about an event so minuscule that neither of us will remember it the next day, or have we allowed ourselves to overlook each other's minor faults in exchange for a loving word? It really isn't much fun to be around someone who is always worrying. Have I allowed myself to become too worried over a church matter that was here today and gone tomorrow, or have I spent my time wisely pursuing eternal values?

Think of the things that have worried you over the last twenty-four hours. Were they worth the time and agony you spent on them? Will anyone remember them one week, or one month from now? If not, you may be guilty of majoring in the minors of life.

Ask the Lord to give you his understanding of what is important. As you begin to view your concerns through the mind of Christ Jesus, you will find you no longer have myriad anxious thoughts. Without the lion of worry chronically gnawing away at you, you will be set free to concentrate on your more important tasks of life—ministry and service.

ONE DAY AT A TIME!

Not only do we need to gain a proper perspective on the majors and minors of life in order to cage the lion of worry, we also need to learn to *live one day at a time.* Notice that at the end of Jesus' instructions about worry, he offers this final gem of advice: "Do not be anxious about tomorrow, for tomorrow will be anxious for itself. Let the day's own trouble be sufficient for the day" (Matt. 6:34).

We begin to tame the lion of worry when we make our problems bite-sized—no bigger than we can handle each day. Many times we are guilty of trying to do too much in one day, or month, or year. And often we worry about things that will never happen! It has been said that 90 percent of all we worry about never comes to pass. We mentally cross bridges that do not need to be crossed. No wonder we feel overwhelmed and anxious!

There is a story about an old man who began to cut trees to build a log house.

A friend inquired, "Isn't that a big undertaking for a man of your years?"

The old man replied, "It would be, if I thought of chopping the trees, sawing the logs, skinning the bark, laying the foundation, erecting the walls, putting on the roof, and finishing the inside along with the doors and windows. Carrying the load all at once would exhaust me. But it isn't so hard to cut down this one tree, and that is all I have to do today."

The late Roy L. Smith tells of his unusual fear of the dark when he was small. One evening after dark when his father asked him to go to the barn for some tools, he had to confess that he was fearful.

Putting a lantern in the boy's hand, his father asked, "How far can you see, son?"

"As far as the mulberry tree."

"Then go out to the mulberry tree."

When the boy arrived there, his father asked, "Now, how far can you see?"

"I can see to the currant bushes," he replied.

When the boy arrived at the currant bushes, his father asked, "How far can you see from there?"

This time it was the henhouse. Next it was the hog lot, and finally the barn.

Step by step, as the boy worked his way to the barn, he replaced his worry with a realization that the dark held nothing he should fear.

In the same way, we can minimize our daily worries by not adding anticipated problems, what ifs, and bogus concerns. Many of these never materialize!

My wife, Ann, recently gave a church-wide talk, "The Bethlehems in My Life." In it, she mentioned the pitfalls of worrying about future concerns which rarely become realized.

> I grew up believing that true Christians were *supposed* to worry. My mother and grandmother, my closest model Christians, worried about everything.

On a beautiful sunny day, we might leave the house for a drive in the country. My grandmother would spot one small cloud in the sky, and say: "Oh, I'm worried a storm is coming." So we would return anxiously to the house and close all the windows.

If we were going to travel on a train to visit relatives, we began to worry a day or two before that we might miss the train. Every school morning, we worried that I might be late for school, and "how awful that would be!" (In all my years of school, I never remember being late.) I was taught to have great anxiety over school grades and tests. If we heard that someone down the road or in town was sick, we worried that we might get sick tomorrow or next week.

We spent our lives worrying about matters that usually never happened. We lived the philosophy, "worry about tomorrow, and add those worries to today"! As a result, by the time I was seventeen years old, I was a champion worrier.

How humorously pathetic, but knowingly familiar! The only way I know that we can counter worrisome attitudes of this kind is to begin to counter them with a new attitude of taking one day at a time. It may take a conscious change of habit on our part to learn to do this, but the rewards are worth it! We *can* learn, step by step, to break down a magnitudinous, uncontrollable problem into one of minute, manageable proportions. When we find ourselves lapsing into anxious thoughts of "what if," "suppose," or "maybe," we *can* immediately stop and ask ourselves if these are legitimate cares which our Lord would have us be concerned about today.

Usually, "what if," "suppose," and "maybe" are red-flag words that should be avoided at all costs! The late Peter Marshall— a famed Presbyterian minister in Washington, D. C.—once published a sermon about "The Problem of Falling Rocks." He believed that the signs Beware of Falling Rocks are of little value when you are driving down the road. If a rock is going to fall, it will fall! There is nothing you can do about it! You can worry that a rock will fall; in fact, you could live your whole life driving down that marked road, looking for rocks that might begin to fall. But in the end, you can do nothing about it should a rock decide to fall, and all your worried, anxious thoughts will be in vain:

> The worrying of the driver has no effect upon the rock, but it has
>   a tremendous effect on the driver.
> People have never fully realized just how destructive a thing
>   worry is.
> It truly plays havoc with one's life.
>   It ruins digestion.
>   It causes stomach ulcers.
>   It interferes with sound sleep and forces us
>   to face another day unrested and irritable.
> It shortens our tempers and makes us snap at the members of our
>   family.[1]

Worry is destructive! But we have a conscious choice. We can look for "falling rocks"—events that might come to pass, but probably never will—but there is nothing we can do to prevent them from coming. We can worry about tomorrow, asking "what if," "suppose," "maybe," to be sure we have covered all the worry bases. Or we can take one day at a time. We can deal with the problems and hassles and worries of life bit by bit, step by step. And in so doing, we begin to defeat the low-spirited lion of worry.

I HAVE TOO MANY BAD HABITS!

Ultimately, if we really want to get a strong grip on the lion of worry, we must deal with its supporting base—*lack of faith in the sovereignty of God.* When we cultivate attitudes of chronic and unnecessary worry, we undermine who God is and what God is about. We narrow our vision and potential in life.

How limiting and harassing the attitude of worry becomes in

our lives if we allow it to remain! Let's face it: Worry habits show our lack of trust in a loving and sovereign God. Worry habits highlight a person who is more self-centered than God-centered; they focus on fear rather than on faith. So in reality, worry is a sin. When we surrender worry to Jesus, we are on our way to conquering this lion.

At one time my middle daughter and her husband, a United Methodist minister, struggled with the lion of worry. Do you remember Hurricane Hugo, which hit the East Coast with great fury in September 1989? The church my son-in-law pastored was right in the path of the hurricane. For three hours, my daughter, her husband, and their two young children huddled in the church basement and fortunately were unhurt! The parsonage where they lived was hit by a twister, and some of the beautiful trees in the yard were uprooted, taking the septic system with them! The chimney, a porch, and a utility-room wall were damaged when one of the huge trees fell on the house. To complicate matters, before it was safe to get back into the parsonage, looters had a picnic!

My daughter and her family were understandably dismayed. And so were the church members. They reacted with worrisome questions: *What if* the insurance would not cover the needed repairs? *Suppose* the looters return? We *should have* put some money aside for a rainy day. *Maybe* we can't handle all the repairs right now. *There's no way* our church can come up with the money we need! The situation became so bad that the district superintendent suggested that the family might have to move their beds to the church fellowship hall and set up house there!

It would have been easy to allow the worry to make the situation a debilitating nightmare for all concerned. Ultimately, the church members rallied. The leaders realized their two options: Take care of the problems as soon as possible; or lament their bad fortune, bemoan the fact that there was limited money to cover the losses, and delay a solution. The leaders chose the first option. They rented a house for my daughter and her family and began to make the needed repairs to the parsonage.

If the church members had allowed their worrisome attitudes to thrive, their witness in the community could have been diminished. A chronic spirit of worry could have limited their potential for accomplishing great things. Instead of moving forward with great faith, they could have let fear and smallness dictate their decisions. By choosing to move forward even in the midst of worrisome circumstances, the church showed faith in a sovereign God's provision for them.

None of us wants to live surrounded by the spirit of worry. We can exchange worry for faith when we make Christ the Lord of our lives. We can fill our lives with trust when we turn them over to Jesus Christ. When we know God is in charge of our lives, we no longer need to take charge ourselves. When problems come our way, we don't need to carry the burden. Jesus offers us a choice:

Come to me, all who labor and are heavy laden, and I will give you rest. Take my yoke upon you, and learn from me; for I am gentle and lowly in heart, and you will find rest for your souls. For my yoke is easy, and my burden is light. (Matt. 11:28-30)

The apostle Paul summed up our choice between worry and faith:

We are afflicted in every way, but not crushed; perplexed, but not driven to despair; persecuted, but not forsaken; struck down, but not destroyed; always carrying in the body the death of Jesus, so that the life of Jesus may also be manifested in our bodies. (II Cor. 4:8-10)

Paul had every reason to worry. His circumstances would have provoked anyone to anxiety and despair. Happily, he knew the secret for downing the lion of worry: His hope and trust were set in Christ Jesus. Paul knew that his circumstances and his very life were in the hands of a sovereign God. His God could handle anything that came his way.

We can rejoice with Paul in that same hope and faith. We can rejoice that we have a great cloud of witnesses to help us run the race of life. Worrisome situations will come our way, but God in Christ can give us new attitudes and hope to deal with whatever comes. We can turn worry from a destructive nightmare into a terrific training ground for faith and hope. We can pray about each and every situation that comes our way, rolling each burden into the loving hands of Jesus. Our faith will be the weapon with which we can defeat the lion of worry, and we can live our lives in peace and tranquility.

Have no anxiety about anything, but in everything by prayer and supplication with thanksgiving let your requests be made known to God. And the peace of God, which passes all understanding, will keep your hearts and your minds in Christ Jesus. (Phil. 4:6-7)

JOURNAL JOTS

For Fun: I could have won first place in the Champion Worrier Contest when:

_____

For Discovery: The Bible addresses many of the same worries we experience today. How did each Old Testament character handle the worries he or she faced?

WORRY	RELATED SCRIPTURE
Does God know what is best for my life?	Abraham's Test: Genesis 22:1-19
What good can come from such bad circumstances in my life?	Joseph's Dilemma: Genesis 45:4-13
Can I trust God's Word to be true?	Moses' Revelation: Exodus 3:13-17
Does God hear my prayers?	Hannah's Desire: I Samuel 1:1-28
What if something bad happens to me?	Elijah's Discovery: I Kings 19:9-18
Has God deserted me in my moment of despair?	Ezekiel's Vision: Ezekiel 37:11-14
What does God want me to do with my life?	David's Realization: Psalm 37:3-5

For Commitment This Week: The thing I am worried about in my life right now:

_____

Read Psalms 71:19-21 and 91:1-16. What words of hope and faith do they offer to help me slay the lion of worry? _____

_____

The Lion of Guilt
Backpacks and Briefcases

PERSONAL INVENTORY: What makes you feel guilty?

Rank each of the following on the Scale of Guilt:

1. would not make me feel guilty at all.
2. would make me feel a little guilty.
3. would make me feel very guilty.

_____ Being irritable with a family member

_____ Cheating on an exam

_____ Losing my temper with a co-worker

_____ Forgetting a close friend's birthday

_____ Not making it to church on Sunday

_____ Spending money on something for myself

_____ Fudging on my IRS return

_____ Procrastinating on daily chores

_____ Eating too much

_____ Neglecting my Bible study and prayer time

_____ Taking a vacation

The Lion of Guilt

_____ Sleeping late on Saturday morning

_____ Feeling jealous of a friend's accomplishments

LIGHTWEIGHT LOADS

I really love to travel! Heaven on earth for me is to have the chance to visit anywhere in the world. But I've learned one thing about traveling: Don't take too many suitcases! It's no fun carrying around dead weights!

Backpacking is much the same. Have you ever seen a hiker carrying a heavy weight? No way! He carries only the essentials—a bit of food, a change of clothes, a first-aid kit, and a tent or sleeping bag. Even the backpack itself is lightweight!

Traveling is easier when you carry one suitcase rather than five. Hiking is more fun when you hoist a lighter load. Life is much more fulfilling when you don't carry around the added burden of unresolved guilt. It is difficult to go through life with a heavy lion of guilt on your back.

Exactly what *is* unresolved guilt? Well, it is . . .

- the baggage of past failures and mistakes;
- the residue that limits hope in our lives;
- the hindrance that keeps us from right relationships with God and others.

WHAT A MESS I'M IN!

> They have all gone astray, they are all alike corrupt;
>   there is none that does good,
>   no, not one. (Ps. 14:3)

> All we like sheep have gone astray;
>   we have turned every one to his own way;
> and the LORD has laid on him
>   the iniquity of us all. (Isa. 53:6)

127

Living in the Lions' Den

Since all have sinned and fall short of the glory of God.
(Rom. 3:23)

The above passages of Scripture sure hit home! I can identify with them—for myself, my family, my church members, and my society. Sin is universal. There is no escaping it. We can't get around it. Sin wreaks havoc in our lives. It causes us to behave like the five-year-old boy in a kindergarten class. The teacher had taught the class to sing a "Popcorn Song." On the chorus, the children were supposed to squat and then "pop up." The teacher noticed that one little boy stayed squatting down on the floor through the entire song, instead of popping up with the others.

She looked at him and asked, "What's wrong with you?"

He replied, "I'm burning on the bottom of the pan!"

Sin often makes us feel as if we are "burning on the bottom of the pan." Guilt, a by-product of our being less than we ought to be, comes from the way we perceive sin. Two factors influence our attitude toward sin:

1. Our conscience—shaped mainly in early childhood by our parents and our church, and later by our peers.
2. God's Word—as we read it and hear it interpreted.

A conscience shaped by Christian people and Christian values has great value. The measure of guilt it generates in a person's life serves one important positive function: It keeps us in line when we begin to stray. It draws boundary lines and sets limits for our behavior. It influences our deeds and actions.

It is only when we allow it to falsely accuse us that guilt takes on a negative demeanor. Only when we carry unresolved guilt and allow it to weigh us down, does it lose its positive perspective and have a crippling, arthritic effect on our lives.

STOP PLAYING GAMES!

In order to keep guilt from becoming a devouring lion, we must learn to *confront our sin.* We cannot ignore it or make it less malignant. We must take responsibility for our sin in all its ugliness. Paul said:

> I see in my members another law at war with the law of my mind and making me captive to the law of sin which dwells in my members. Wretched man that I am! Who will deliver me from this body of death? (Rom. 7:23-24)

Most of the time, we can correctly assess our sin and initial guilt. We recognize that we have broken one of God's laws or disobeyed godly instruction. We have broken faith with God, with others, and with ourselves. We feel guilty about our wrongdoing, and rightly so.

But there is another side to the coin of guilt. Sometimes we may be carrying false guilt. That is, we may feel guilty for something that was not our fault or was beyond our control. My youngest daughter is good at assuming false guilt. If someone in the family acts thoughtlessly toward her, she soon will be apologizing to that person for hurting *her* feelings!

In another form of false guilt, we may have confessed our sin to God but continue to feel guilty. Though God has wiped the slate clean, we continue to punish ourselves for our mistake.

If you are having difficulty distinguishing sin from false guilt, you may need an outside party—a trusted friend, your pastor, or a family member—to help you sort things out. Once you have isolated your sin, confess it head-on. Say, "Lord Jesus, here I am, in all my ugliness. I cannot deny my sinfulness. I need your forgiveness."

Fortunately, the story does not end here. Once we have confessed our guilt we open the floodgates, and God's love, mercy, grace, and forgiveness can pour into us and out to others. The lion of guilt need not have a feast at our expense.

I AM WHAT I THINK I AM?

Confronting and confessing our sin is the first step toward removing unwanted guilt from our lives. *Restoration* is the natural second step. When we can offer remediation to others for our reckless ways, it becomes easier for us to forget our past mistakes and move forward positively.

Restoration is a threefold response. First, we need to be able to view our actions and responses through the eyes of the affected person.

My daughter and her family had an interesting experience one summer. They spent a couple of weeks with a college student who thought he could live for weeks at a time without committing a single sin. In fact, he perceived his behavior as flawless during the weeks my daughter and her family were with him. The ironic thing about his perception was that my daughter's emotions had been in a turmoil for the entire visit. She perceived the young man as cocky, interfering, and lazy. When she and the young man compared notes at the end of the visit, each was astounded at the other's feelings!

Becoming sensitive to the feelings and opinions of others is important before we can make restitution. By talking with them, trying to understand things from their perspective, and watching for clues from their responses to us, we can begin the process of restoration.

Once we assess our own erring behavior, we can continue the process of restoration by offering words of apology. Why is it so hard for some of us to say "I'm sorry"? Often we are too proud! We think we should not admit our weaknesses to someone else. How ridiculous! We need to practice daily those important words, "I'm sorry," and speak them appropriately. There is no reason to feel guilty and yet refuse to rectify the situation. If you will speak these healing words, others usually will respond with love and forgiveness.

There are some exceptions which may preclude apologizing to the offended party. For instance, if the offended person is unaware of what happened, it would simply cause unnecessary grief to inform the person of the hurtful act you committed, in the name of "clearing your conscience." In this instance, confession to God in prayer or, if absolutely necessary, to an uninvolved third party such as your pastor, would be much more advisable.

ZACCHAEUS WAS A WEE LITTLE MAN!

Recognizing our failures and verbalizing an apology are good starts. But restoration also involves a practical response.

Think about the first-century tax collector Zacchaeus. He felt compelled to make restitution to those he had wronged. He wanted to pass on to others the mercy that Jesus had shown him.

And Zacchaeus stood and said to the Lord, "Behold, Lord, the half of my goods I give to the poor; and if I have defrauded any one of anything, I restore it fourfold."

And Jesus said to him, "Today salvation has come to this house, since he also is a son of Abraham. For the Son of man came to seek and to save the lost." (Luke 19:8-10)

Zacchaeus' example is a good one for us to follow. He didn't sit around punishing himself for his past greediness. He confessed his sin. He let go of it in exchange for something better. Then he followed up his new commitment by concrete action: He restored to those he had defrauded.

How much we can learn from Zacchaeus! If you have committed a wrong toward someone, ask God's forgiveness, ask the injured person's forgiveness, and then make it right.

Are you fudging in your business affairs? Confess your sin and change your ways. As much as possible, settle with those you have cheated.

Have you thoughtlessly injured a friend? Go to that person and apologize. Ask the Lord to help you to be more sensitive in the future.

Have you neglected your relationship with a family member? Determine right away to reconcile with that loved one. Write a letter or pick up the telephone. If possible, restore family relationships with immediacy.

One final word about the process of restoration: Don't delay! Restoration takes time and effort; it usually is not accomplished overnight. You may need to enlist the support of your pastor or a dependable friend to help you get started and stay on course. Life is too short to fill it with guilt. Determine to change today, with God's help!

HANGIN' ON!

Confession and restoration are important weapons in taming the lion of guilt. Ultimately, however, we must be willing to *close the gate* on our guilt, if we are to render the lion powerless. When we close the gate on guilt—letting old guilt go, leaving lingering guilt behind the gate—only then will we open the door to new life and new possibilities.

Letting go of our guilt can be very difficult. A priest told about a woman who used to come every week for confession. She would list her sins, and every Saturday he would forgive her in Jesus' name.

Finally, after weeks of hearing her confess the same litany of sins, he said to her, "Woman, I cannot absolve you of these sins."

She looked surprised. "Why not? You've forgiven me every week."

He responded, "But woman, you are to commit them no more!"

"I know that," she replied. "These are sins I committed in the past."

"When did you commit these sins?" the priest asked.

"Many years ago."

"Why do you continue to confess them?"

"Well, I just don't let them go."

Then he told her, "You must confess them and remember them no more, if you would be set free from old guilt. You must close the door on yesterday in order to have a better tomorrow."

Jonah didn't want to let go of his guilt, either. Somehow, it was easier for him to flee from God than to face his disobedience squarely, confess it, let it go, and get on about the business of ministry. Finally, in the deep abyss of the belly of the whale, Jonah faced up to his sin and closed the gate on his guilt.

> When my soul fainted within me,
>   I remembered the Lord;
> and my prayer came to thee,
>   into thy holy temple.
> Those who pay regard to vain idols
>   forsake their true loyalty.
> But I with the voice of thanksgiving
>   will sacrifice to thee;
> what I have vowed I will pay. (Jon. 2:7-9)

Paul is a good example of someone who was able to confess his sin and let go of the accompanying guilt. He could have pretended that he had never persecuted Christians. He could have chastised himself over his past sins and not accepted God's forgiveness. Instead, he chose to let go of his past sins and accept the new life God offered him.

> So Ananias departed and entered the house. And laying his hands on him he said, "Brother Saul, the Lord Jesus who appeared to you on the road by which you came, has sent me that you may regain your sight and be filled with the Holy Spirit." And immediately something like scales fell from his eyes and he regained his sight. Then he rose and was baptized, and took food and was strengthened.
>
> For several days he was with the disciples at Damascus. And in the synagogues *immediately* he proclaimed Jesus, saying, "He is the Son of God." (Acts 9:17-20, italics mine)

We can close the gate to lingering guilt more easily when we are honest with ourselves. I learned this firsthand while still in seminary. Although I was thankful that I had been brought up in a Christian home, I worried because there was no "Damascus Road experience" in my past. One day I determined to settle the issue with certainty once and for all. I told the Lord, "I know there have been a lot of people worse than I have been, and many who have been better, but I come before you just as I am. I give my life to you completely, to use as you will. I'm ready to press on to higher ground."

Do you know that God has not brought up my yesterdays since? As I closed the gate on old feelings of inadequacy, I opened a door to a new room, full of spiritual treasures. By facing my guilt honestly, I began to carry a lighter load in my backpack of life.

I want to mention one other thought about letting go of our guilt. Often, saying we are letting go and doing it are two different things. I know a fine Christian counselor who has a good analogy to help bridge that dichotomy. When we have old guilt we need to remove from our lives, imagine that we place all of it on a bed sheet and that the sheet is tied together by its four corners and lifted heavenward. In this way, we mentally release our guilt to God.

Peter had a similar vision. He saw a great sheet full of all kinds of animals which came down from heaven. A voice instructed him to "rise, Peter; kill and eat." But Peter said,

> "No, Lord; for I have never eaten anything that is common or unclean." And the voice came to him again a second time, "What God has cleansed, you must not call common." This happened three times, and the thing was taken up at once to heaven. (Acts 10:14-16)

The vision enabled Peter to release all his previous thoughts and customs heavenward. He offered his prejudices and past feelings to God, and his life was changed. And we can use the same analogy effectively in our lives.

If you tend to carry heavy suitcases of guilt wherever you go, try laying them before God. Then picture God gently but totally grasping their handles and lifting them out of your reach. You no longer need to carry them. You are free from the burden of the extra weight which encumbers you, keeps you from right living and satisfying relationships.

FROM GUILT TO GRACE

Exchanging suitcases for backpacks requires that we confront our sins, make restoration to those we have wronged, and close the gate on any lingering guilt. Sometimes this is an overnight process. More frequently, changing old habits takes time. As we open the door to the bounties God has prepared for us, guilt gradually is replaced by grace. We shift from guilt to grace as we seek God's upward calling in our lives.

We often underrate the best that God has for us. The story of a little boy who came home after the last day of school vividly depicts this. He proudly showed his mother the ribbon he had received in the awards assembly and said excitedly, "Mom, I got *horrible* mention!"

We need not settle for "horrible" mention in our lives. We don't need to carry a heavy load of unresolved guilt everywhere we go. God offers us awards of *honorable* mention. He calls us to put our past behind us and move forward with great joy. We can move from guilt to grace.

Isn't that what the disciples did after the resurrection of Jesus? They had betrayed Jesus several days earlier; they had deserted their beloved Master. They were filled with remorse, humiliation, guilt. But Jesus' response was one of grace. He appeared to them three times, as recounted in the Gospel of John, and each time he offered forgiveness, restoration, and new hope:

Jesus said to them again, "Peace be with you. As the Father has sent me, even so I send you." (John 20:21)

Eight days later . . . Jesus came and stood among them, and said, "Peace be with you." Then he said to Thomas, "Put your finger here, and see my hands; and put out your hand, and place it in my side; do not be faithless, but believing." (John 20:26-27)

[Jesus] said to [Peter] the third time, "Simon, son of John, do you love me?" Peter was grieved because he said to him the third time, "Do you love me?" And he said to him, "Lord, you know everything; you know that I love you." Jesus said to him, "Feed my sheep." (John 21:17)

A SECOND CHANCE

Many years ago, a convicted sheep thief was punished by receiving a branded ST (Sheep Thief) on his forehead. One particular thief who was so marked knew that the only way he could begin anew was to stay in his hometown and prove to those who knew him as a sheep thief that he could be something better. He began to give unselfishly, to help others, and to build his character above reproach.

Many years and many good deeds later, a young child noticed the letters on the man's forehead and quizzed her mother, "What does ST mean?"

As her mother reflected upon the man's new character, she replied, "Honey, I guess it means *saint!*"

By the grace of God, we are the sheep thieves who can become saints. God, through Calvary, calls us to a better way. We can confess, restore, let go, and move forward. There is a divine answer for every remaining guilt in our lives. Either God in Christ died for our sins, or he didn't. There's no need to straddle the fence. We can exchange our suitcases for backpacks and briefcases; we can exchange our guilt for God's grace.

There is therefore now no condemnation for those who are in Christ Jesus. For the law of the Spirit of life in Christ Jesus has set me free from the law of sin and death. (Rom. 8:1-2)

JOURNAL JOTS

For Fun: The first time in my life I remember feeling guilty was:

_____

For Discovery: Examine the following biblical persons who experienced feelings of guilt. What incidents caused their guilt? How did they resolve it?
1. Jacob (Gen. 27–28)
2. Joseph (Gen. 37, 45)
3. Moses (Exod. 2:11–3:22)
4. David (II Sam. 11–12:24; Ps. 51)
5. Woman of the city (Luke 7:36-50)
6. Samaritan woman (John 4:1-42)
7. Woman caught in adultery (John 8:2-11)
8. Judas (Matt. 27:3-10)

For Commitment This Week: Make a list of any unresolved guilt you carry in your life. Spend some time in prayer about this, so you can make your list as complete as possible. Now take each area of guilt and consider the four "helps":
1. confrontation
2. letting go
3. restoration
4. moving on

Which "help" is the most difficult for you to implement?

_____

Which is the easiest? _____

_____

Now choose one area to begin to change from guilt to grace this week. The area(s) I have chosen: _____

The Lion of Doubt

Hanging On by a Mustard Seed

PERSONAL INVENTORY: How tough are you?

1. You have just heard that a close Christian friend has been diagnosed with terminal cancer. The person is young and has two small children. Your response . . .
   a) toward your friend is _____
   b) toward your friend's family is _____
   c) toward God is _____
   d) within yourself is _____

2. You have just been laid off of your job. It's no fault of your own; in fact, you are a conscientious worker. Your response . . .
   a) toward your boss is _____
   b) toward co-workers is _____
   c) toward God is _____
   d) within yourself is _____

3. A scandal has occurred at your church. Members of the church begin to take sides, with anger, hurt, and name-calling the inevitable by-products. Your response: _____

4. Think of a crisis that has happened in your life in the last two years. Has your faith grown or diminished as a result?

Why?

I SURE COULD USE A LITTLE HELP!

The phone rang late one night at the house. "Jane," a church member, was on the line. She was at the end of her rope. Her teenage children caused her nothing but trouble. Her marriage was crumbling. Her job was full of intense pressure. Her husband's business was near bankruptcy. The more she prayed, the worse her circumstances seemed to grow.

She pleaded, "Brother Paul, I feel as if I'm losing my faith. Can you help me?"

THE INTERSTATE BABY

If we are honest, all of us have such feelings from time to time. I remember the experience of my middle daughter when she was expecting her second baby.

After the difficult birth of her first child, she had taken every precaution for smoother sailing in anticipation of the second birth. She carefully selected her doctor and hospital, and began the long wait!

Despite attention to every detail, things hardly went as expected. Three and a half weeks before her scheduled C-section, she and her husband traveled to a nearby city to do some last-minute baby shopping. As they walked in the door of the department store, her membranes ruptured, and she went into labor. Here she was, in sudden unexpected labor, and a two-hour drive from her doctor and hospital!

Her husband quickly hurried her back to their car, and they immediately set out for home. He figured that the faster they drove, the quicker they might capture a highway patrol's attention, and thus receive a police escort to their hospital. Sure enough, within a few miles a patrolman pulled them over, but insisted that they return in a local ambulance to the city they had just left! It took an hour for the ambulance to arrive on the scene! By the time they finally got to the hospital, my daughter was in active labor and strong panic. You can only imagine the state of her husband!

As the strange doctor and unfamiliar hospital staff began hurried preparations for her surgery, my daughter asked the ever-eternal and unanswered questions we all have thrown up to God at one time or another:

- Where are you in *this*, God? Have you forgotten about me?
- Why me, Lord? What have I done? Are all my plans to be in vain?

Even I, as a grandparent, wondered what plan God was following in that situation!

THE BIGGEST LION OF ALL

King David experienced some of these same feelings of helplessness and doubt in uncertain circumstances.

> Be merciful to me, O God, be merciful to me,
>   for in thee my soul takes refuge;
> in the shadow of thy wings I will take refuge,
>   till the storms of destruction pass by.
> I cry to God Most High,
>   to God who fulfills his purpose for me.
> He will send from heaven and save me,
>   he will put to shame those who trample upon me.
> God will send forth his steadfast love and his faithfulness!

The Lion of Doubt

I lie in the *midst of lions*
    that greedily devour the sons of men;
their teeth are spears and arrows,
    their tongues sharp swords. . . .
Let thy glory be over all the earth!
(Ps. 57:1-5; a Miktam of David, when he fled from
Saul; italics mine.)

Just like King David, each and every one of us is affected by the lions of stress. Busyness, career decisions, finances, family relationships, and unchecked emotions are the lions we wrestle every day. The one thing that can keep us going and give us hope and strength to face our daily problems is our faith in God. But what can we do when *even* God seems far away? How do we respond to the "wilderness" times in our lives? What can we do when doubt seeps in?

I WISH I COULD BE SURE OF EVERYTHING!

Don't you love to open a present? The wrapping paper fits so neatly around the box that holds your treasure. The bow is tied just right around the package. What a neat, tidy gift, just waiting for you to open it!

But life isn't like that! You can't tie circumstances up in a neat package of resolutions. Out-go doesn't always match up with in-come. Cause doesn't necessarily mesh with effect. And often, life is just not fair!

Being a Christian in today's uncertain world isn't easy. When life deals us a bad blow, it's easy to blame God. Our faith can take a beating when the lions of stress attack us. In times like these, we can easily wonder if being a Christian pays any dividends at all.

How can we build our faith in times of trouble? How can we learn to dispel our doubt in adverse situations? How can we deal with negative circumstances and still "keep the faith"?

THE MUSTARD SEED

One way to get rid of doubt in troublesome times is to *activate a mustard-seed dose of faith* in our lives. Have you ever seen a mustard seed? In the Holy Land, you can buy a mustard seed encased in a tiny glass pendant. That's about the only way you can see the seed, it's so minute—much smaller than a pinhead. Yet Jesus told his followers that a mustard-seed dose of faith, acted upon, was more than enough to accomplish great things: "If you had faith as a grain of mustard seed, you could say to this sycamore tree, 'Be rooted up, and be planted in the sea,' and it would obey you" (Luke 17:6).

Sometimes we think that faith must be of great magnitude. But Jesus rewarded even the smallest measure of faith, while encouraging those persons to exercise and develop their faith even more.

Early in his ministry, Jesus accepted and encouraged the small faith of Simon Peter. Jesus said to him:

"Put out into the deep and let down your nets for a catch." And Simon answered, "Master, we toiled all night and took nothing! But at your word I will let down the nets."

And when they had done this, they enclosed a great shoal of fish; and as their nets were breaking, they beckoned to their partners in the other boat to come and help them. And they came and filled both the boats, so that they began to sink.

But when Simon Peter saw it, he fell down at Jesus' knees, saying, "Depart from me, for I am a sinful man, O Lord." For he was astonished, and all that were with him, at the catch of fish which they had taken. . . .

And Jesus said to Simon, "Do not be afraid; henceforth you will be catching men." And when they had brought their boats to land, they left everything and followed him. (Luke 5:4-11)

Jesus gave Simon Peter the simple challenge to let down his nets in faith, so that Jesus could fill them with fish. Then he gave

Peter an even greater challenge of faith: He told him that soon he would be about the more important task of sharing the gospel with others.

Jesus also responded directly to the small faith of Thomas, by accepting it and building upon it:

> "Put your finger here, and see my hands; and put out your hand, and place it in my side; do not be faithless, but believing." Thomas answered him, "My Lord and my God!" Jesus said to him, "Have you believed because you have seen me? Blessed are those who have not seen and yet believe." (John 20:27-29)

Jesus could have chastised Thomas for not being present with the other disciples when he had appeared to them earlier. He could have questioned Thomas's loyalty, but instead, he met Thomas at his point of need. He took the little bit of faith that Thomas had and built upon it.

Just as Jesus met Simon Peter and Thomas at their points of need, our Lord meets us as we exercise our small faith. He asks us to give him a chance. He understands that we will have some doubts. It's what we do with the bit of faith we have that counts. Jesus, our lion of Judah, overcomes our lions of doubt through our faith.

WHEN THE GOING GETS TOUGH, THE TOUGH GET GOING.

Not only do we need to activate a mustard-seed dose of faith, but there are times when we must *hang on to it with great tenacity.* Three characters in the book of Daniel—Shadrach, Meshach, and Abednego—give us a model for keeping the faith as we deal with negative circumstances. Those men *set their minds resolutely to trust God, no matter what the outcome.*

Remember the story? King Nebuchadnezzar of Babylon

commanded all persons in the nation to fall down and worship the golden image he had made. But three Jewish men—Shadrach, Meshach, and Abednego—paid no attention to the decree. Nebuchadnezzar became furious and ordered that they be put into a fiery furnace. Despite this ugly situation, they made very clear to the king that their trust in God would not be swayed, even if they perished:

> O Nebuchadnezzar, we have no need to answer you in this matter. If it be so, our God whom we serve is able to deliver us from the burning fiery furnace, and he will deliver us out of your hand, O king. But *if not*, be it known to you, O king, that we will not serve your gods or worship the golden image which you have set up. (Dan. 3:16-18, italics mine)

God ultimately resolved the problem by delivering them from the furnace unsinged. But the important focus of the story is not upon the outcome, but upon the resolute trust in God of the three in the midst of their ordeal. They made clear to King Nebuchadnezzar that no matter what action God took, they would be faithful to their Lord. Their faith was not dependent upon God's performance.

Consider the story of Daniel in the den of lions. His circumstances would have provoked anyone to doubt. Yet he set his hope steadfastly upon God, even facing a crowd of hungry lions. Although God shut the mouths of the lions and Daniel remained unharmed, his fate is secondary to his steadfast trust in God. He continued to do the right thing—worship his God—even though he knew it could mean his life (see Dan. 6).

Simon Peter also set his face resolutely toward God. King Herod had arrested him and thrown him in jail, probably intending to put him to death, just as he had slain James the brother of John (see Acts 12:1-3). Peter surely must have wondered if this was his time to die! James, an equally faithful servant, had just been murdered. Would Peter's fate be the same?

The Scriptures answer that question with a resounding No!

Peter's fate was not the same as James' at that point. God's providence was not yet finished with Peter and his mission on earth. Acts tells us of his exciting rescue from prison:

> The very night when Herod was about to bring him out, Peter was sleeping between two soldiers, bound with two chains, and sentries before the door were guarding the prison; and behold, an angel of the Lord appeared, and a light shone in the cell; and he struck Peter on the side and woke him, saying, "Get up quickly." And the chains fell off his hands. (Acts 12:6-7)

Again, the outcome of Peter's circumstance is not nearly as important as his attitude before and during his arrest. He steadfastly trusted God, in spite of the unnerving circumstances. Even though he could not foresee the future result, he kept his faith in God.

The Columbian missionary Bruce Olson is a contemporary example of resolute trust in God in the midst of harrowing experiences. For nine months, Bruce was a political prisoner of guerrilla leaders. He was subjected to a variety of emotional and physical tortures, culminating with being tied to a tree and fired at with machine guns. At first he considered himself dead, yet alive to God. But he soon realized that the men were firing blanks, that this was one more psychological torture he was being forced to undergo.

A few weeks after that incident, Bruce was miraculously set free. How was he able to keep his faith under such distress? In his own words, he gives us some clues:

> It never once occurred to me that it was God's responsibility to rescue me miraculously from this situation. Instead, I believed it was my responsibility to serve Him right where I was. What I asked of God from day to day was very simple . . . "Father, I'm alive and I want to use this time constructively. How can I be useful to you today?" . . . Even when I couldn't see or hear what He was doing, I could trust that He was always there. . . . I knew

it was God—not my captors—who would control the outcome of the situation.[1]

THE OTHER SIDE OF THE COIN

So far, these examples have been heroes who were faithful to God in the midst of negative circumstances. God moved miraculously and changed their situations for the better.

But the "roll call" in the book of Hebrews tells the other side: There were equally heroic figures whose faithfulness to God resulted in torture and death.

> Some were tortured, refusing to accept release, that they might rise again to a better life. Others suffered mocking and scourging, and even chains and imprisonment. They were stoned, they were sawn in two, they were killed with the sword; they went about in skins of sheep and goats, destitute, afflicted, ill-treated—of whom the world was not worthy—wandering over deserts and mountains, and in dens and caves of the earth. (Heb. 11:35-38)

The point the Scripture seems to be making, in all these examples, is that negative circumstances will come the way of all Christians. It may seem that God has deserted you; and if your faith is dependent upon the positive outcome of these circumstances, doubt is sure to rise within you. But if you resolutely set your hope and trust in God, independent of the circumstantial lions that rage about you, your faith will grow. Apparently, the outcome of the circumstance is not the important factor. It's how we respond to God in the heat of the hour that counts.

The late Catherine Marshall, in *A Closer Walk*, describes the importance of a tenacious spirit of faith in the midst of trouble:

> Total all-out trust on our part is not as easy as it first seems. There are periods when God's face is shrouded, when His dealings with us will appear as if He does not care, when He seems not to be

acting like a true Father. Can we then hang onto the fact of His love and His faithfulness and that He is a prayer-answering God?

Can we get to the point Habakkuk reached: "Though the fig tree does not blossom, and there be no fruit on the vines. . . . Yet I will rejoice in the Lord . . . !" (Habakkuk 3:17-18 *Amplified*).

Can we, at the moment when His face is hidden, exult in the God of our salvation? "The Lord God is my strength, my personal bravery and my invincible army" (v. 19). . . .

As the symptoms get worse, the temptation is there to "give up" and not to trust Jesus. We must resist that temptation in the midst of our very real human helplessness, "roll" the entire burden onto His shoulders, as He bade us do, step out and take the first step with bare, no-evidence-at-all, faith.

And lo, He does take over gloriously, doing what we literally cannot do for ourselves.[2]

THE CROSSROADS

A tenacious spirit of hanging on in the midst of trouble is not something that feels good or is naturally easy to do. Our resolute trust in God is not an emotion. It is a conscious act of our will. We must make an intentional decision to trust Jesus Christ to meet our needs and give us direction in life.

A friend of mine aptly expressed the choice we have as Christians: "In the midst of a crisis, I wonder if being a Christian is too difficult. And then I think: Where else would I go? Nothing else on earth holds any hope or answers for me besides Jesus Christ."

Isn't that what Simon Peter also expressed when Jesus posed the question, "But who do *you* say that I am?" Peter answered, "You are the Christ, the Son of the Living God" (Matt. 16:15-16). Jesus was calling Peter to resolute trust and commitment. What others thought about Jesus was not important. Even though the storms of life were heading Peter's way, his faith would grow and emerge stronger as he learned to focus on God, rather than on circumstances.

I experienced that when I moved to a new church several years ago. When I arrived, the circumstances were rather bleak. The church was split into several factions because of past hurts, and it seemed that I became the scapegoat for all the mistrust and disillusionment. The healing process was unusually slow, and much of the time it seemed to go backward rather than forward. For two years we made very little progress. It would have been so easy for me to focus on the outward circumstances, to wonder whether this church could ever experience unity under God's loving hand. But hour by hour, day by day, week by week, as I resolutely ignored outward appearances and set my hope and expectation in God, the attitudes and emotions of people in the church began to change. In the end, my growing faith, and that of the congregation, will not be disappointed.

KEEP HANGING IN THERE!

A mustard seed may not seem like much to hang from. But it's a start. It's all that God requires. God can take our tenacious mustard seed of faith and begin to use it to move mountains in our lives, and in the lives of others. Our mustard seed of faith will be enough to keep our trust in God secure in the midst of life's stresses. Our mustard seed of faith will sustain us from any and all the devouring lions we face. We can emerge from the den with renewed faith, just as Daniel did, and we can rejoice in our God, just as King Darius did:

> For he is the living God,
>   enduring for ever;
> his kingdom shall never be destroyed,
>   and his dominion shall be to the end.
> He delivers and rescues,
>   he works signs and wonders
>   in heaven and on earth,
> he who has saved Daniel
>   from the power
>   of the lions. (Dan. 6:26b-27)

JOURNAL JOTS

For Fun: Who was your childhood hero, and why? _____

_____

For Discovery: Read Hebrews 11. Make a list of all the heroes of faith, and some of the circumstances in each of their lives. (Refer to additional passages in the Bible for more details of their lives if you wish.) How did the heroes respond to their given circumstances? What was God's response?

You may want to organize your thoughts in the following way:

HERO	CIRCUMSTANCE	HERO'S RESPONSE	GOD'S RESPONSE

Also read Hebrews 12:22-24. Be aware that when you are going through troubled circumstances, you have many powerful resources available to you. You have the living God, innumerable angels, the assembly of strong witnesses, the sprinkled blood, and Jesus, your High Priest, your Lord and Savior, ever living to make intercession for you (Heb. 7:25).

For Commitment This Week: What is your biggest trial right now? _____

_____

How can you use what you have learned from your trials in the past to give you hope to face your current problem? _____

_____

MORE FOOD FOR THOUGHT

CHAPTER I: THE LION OF BUSYNESS

Glaphre. *When the Pieces Don't Fit . . . God Makes the Difference.* Grand Rapids: Zondervan, 1984.
Kimmel, Tim. *Little House on the Freeway.* Portland, Oreg.: Multnomah Press, 1988.
Peters, Thomas J., and Nancy Austin. *A Passion for Excellence.* New York: Random House, 1985.

CHAPTER II: THE LION OF CAREER

Neef, LaVonne, et al. *Practical Christianity.* Wheaton, Ill.: Tyndale House Publishers, 1987.
Tchividjian, Gigi Graham. *Diapers and Dishes or Pinstripes and Pumps.* Nashville: Thomas Nelson, 1987.

CHAPTER III: THE LION OF FINANCES

Blue, Ron, and Judy Blue. *Money Matters for Parents and Their Kids.* Nashville: Thomas Nelson, Oliver-Nelson, 1988.
Burkett, Larry. *The Complete Financial Guide for Young Couples.* Wheaton, Ill.: Scripture Press, Victor Books, 1989.
Neef, LaVonne, et al. *Practical Christianity.* Wheaton, Ill.: Tyndale House, 1987.
Roberts, Wes; Judy Roberts; and H. Norman Wright. *After You Say "I Do."* Eugene, Oreg.: Harvest House, 1979.

CHAPTER IV: THE LION OF FAMILY RELATIONSHIPS

Dobson, James C. *Straight Talk to Men and Their Wives.* Waco, Tex.: Word Books, 1980.

Owens, Virginia Stem. *A Feast of Families.* New York: Macmillan Publishing Co., 1988.

Young, Helen M. *Children Won't Wait: Parent's Prayer.* Fort Worth, Tex.: Brownlow Publishing Co., 1985.

CHAPTER V: THE LION OF DEPRESSION

Landorf, Joyce. *Silent September.* Waco, Tex.: Word Books, 1984.

Sandford, John, and Paula Sandford. *The Transformation of the Inner Man.* Tulsa, Okla.: Victory House, 1982.

Seamands, David. *Healing for Damaged Emotions.* Wheaton, Ill.: Victor Books, 1981.

Weeks, Claire. *Hope and Help for Your Nerves.* New York: Bantam Books, 1981.

CHAPTER VI: THE LION OF RESENTMENT

Smedes, Lewis B. *Forgive and Forget: Healing the Hurts We Don't Deserve.* San Francisco: Harper & Row, 1984.

Yancey, Philip. *Where Is God When It Hurts?* Grand Rapids: Zondervan, 1977.
———. *Disappointment with God.* Grand Rapids: Zondervan, 1988.

CHAPTER VII: THE LION OF ANGER

Hemfelt, Robert; Frank Minirth; and Paul Meier. *Love Is a Choice.* Nashville: Thomas Nelson, 1989.

Keysor, Charles W. *Living Unafraid.* Elgin, Ill.: David C. Cook Publishing, 1973.

Minirth, Frank, et al. *The Healthy Christian Life.* Grand Rapids: Baker Book House, 1988.

CHAPTER VIII: THE LION OF WORRY

Marshall, Catherine. *A Closer Walk.* ed. Leonard E. LeSourd. New York: Fleming H. Revell, 1986.

Peale, Norman Vincent. *Stop Worrying and Start Living.* Pawling, N.Y.: Foundation for Christian Living, 1982.
Sangster, W. E. *The Pattern of Prayer.* Grand Rapids: Zondervan, Francis Asbury Press, 1988.

CHAPTER IX: THE LION OF GUILT

Carlson, Dwight. *From Guilt to Grace.* Eugene, Oreg.: Harvest House Publishers, 1983.
Clark, Mary Franzen. *Hiding, Hurting, Healing: Restoration for Today's Woman.* Grand Rapids: Zondervan, Francis Asbury Press, 1985.
Dobson, James. *Emotions: Can You Trust Them?* Glendale, Calif.: Regal Books, 1980.

CONCLUSION: THE LION OF DOUBT

Larson, Bruce. *The Presence.* New York: Harper & Row, 1988.
Sangster, W. E. *He Is Able.* Grand Rapids: Zondervan, Francis Asbury Press, 1988.
Schaeffer, Edith. *Affliction.* New York: Fleming H. Revell, 1978.
Yancey, Philip. *Where Is God When It Hurts?* Grand Rapids: Zondervan, 1977.

N   O   T   E   S

CHAPTER I: THE LION OF BUSYNESS

1. David A. Seamands, *Healing Grace* (Wheaton, Ill.: Victor Books, 1988), p. 64.

CHAPTER II: THE LION OF CAREER

1. "Prayer Is the Soul's Sincere Desire," *The Book of Hymns* (Nashville: The United Methodist Publishing House, 1966), p. 252.
2. Louis Harris, *Inside America* (New York: Random House, Vintage Books, 1987), pp. 17-20.
3. Ibid., p. 109.
4. Bill Cosby, *Fatherhood* (New York: Berkley Books, 1986), p. 42.

CHAPTER III: THE LION OF FINANCES

1. See Holley H. Ulbrich and T. Bruce Yandle, Jr., *Managing Personal Finance* (Dallas, Tex.: Business Publications/Georgetown, Ont.: Irwin-Dorsey Ltd., 1979), esp. chap. 4.
2. Quoted in Mike Hall, "Example Trains Children in Financial Management," *The United Methodist Reporter* (April 14, 1989): 5.
3. "The Danger of Increasing Riches," *Through the Year with Wesley*, ed. Frederick C. Gill (Nashville: The Upper Room, 1983), p. 156.

Notes

CHAPTER IV: THE LION OF FAMILY RELATIONSHIPS

1. Alan L. McGinnis, *The Romance Factor* (New York: Harper & Row, 1982), p. 189.
2. Margery Williams, *The Velveteen Rabbit* (New York: Alfred A. Knopf/ Toronto: Random House, 1985), pp. 11-13.
3. James C. Dobson, *The Strong-willed Child* (Wheaton, Ill.: Tyndale House, 1978), pp. 115-16.
4. Bill Cosby, *Fatherhood* (New York: Berkley Books, 1986), pp. 64-65.

CHAPTER V: THE LION OF DEPRESSION

1. Daniel F. Kripke, "Seasonal Affective Disorder and Phototherapy," *Annals of the New York Academy of Sciences* 453 (1985): 260-67.
2. This booklet is a reprint of the chapter from James C. Dobson's *What Wives Wish Their Husbands Knew About Women* (Wheaton, Ill.: Tyndale House, 1975).
3. Louis Harris, *Inside America* (New York: Random House, Vintage Books, 1987), p. 3.
4. Stephen Brown, *When Your Rope Breaks* (Nashville: Thomas Nelson, 1988), pp. 110-11.

CHAPTER VI: THE LION OF RESENTMENT

1. Karen Burton Mains, *With My Whole Heart: Disciplines for Strengthening the Inner Life* (Portland, Oreg.: Multnomah Press, 1982), p. 123.
2. John Sandford and Paula Sandford, *The Transformation of the Inner Man* (Tulsa, Okla.: Victory House, 1982), p. 261. For a more detailed discussion, see chap. 14.
3. Ibid., p. 266.

CHAPTER VII: THE LION OF ANGER

1. Lewis B. Smedes, *Forgive and Forget: Healing the Hurts We Don't Deserve* (San Francisco: Harper & Row, 1984), p. 21.
2. James C. Dobson, *Emotions: Can You Trust Them?* (Ventura, Calif.: Regal Books, 1980), pp. 82-85.

Notes

CHAPTER VIII: THE LION OF WORRY

1. Peter Marshall, *Mr. Jones, Meet the Master* (New York: Fleming H. Revell, 1950), p. 162. For an excellent sermon on the subject of worry, read the whole chapter.

CONCLUSION: THE LION OF DOUBT

1. Bruce Olson, with Susan DeVore Williams, "Hostage," *Charisma and Christian Life* (November 1989): 3.
2. Catherine Marshall, *A Closer Walk*, ed. Leonard E. LeSourd (New York: Fleming H. Revell, 1986), pp. 144-45.